DRAWING THE LARGER CIRCLE

DRAWING THE LARGER CIRCLE

How to Love and Be Loved

Jack and Cornelia Addington

DEVORSS & COMPANY
P.O. Box 550
Marina del Rey, California 90294

CONTENTS

Introduction............................ vii

1 DRAWING THE LARGER CIRCLE........ 1

2 WHAT IS LOVE?..................... 9

3 LOVE IS FREEDOM.................. 20

4 PERFECT LOVE CASTS OUT FEAR....... 30

5 THE LOVE WE GIVE AWAY WE KEEP.... 43

6 LOVE IS THE HEALER OF
MIND AND BODY.................. 52

7 LOVE IS IRRESISTIBLE................ 62

8 LOVE IS FORGIVENESS................ 71

9 GOD'S LOVE IS UNCONDITIONAL..... 86

10 PUTTING LOVE TO WORK
Love Techniques.................... 95

11 GETTING ALONG WITH DIFFICULT PEOPLE
Love Techniques Cont'd............. 104

12 LOVE—THE ANSWER TO EVERY NEED
More Love Techniques.............. 115

13 LOVE TRANSCENDS GUILTS........... 126

14 THE OVERVIEW...................... 136

ACKNOWLEDGMENT

It would be impossible to list here all of the people whose written words inspired this book or all of the people whose true life stories fill its pages.

We do want to mention, however, our long-time secretaries who have contributed endless hours to its completion: Alice Richards, Phyllis Smith-Flajole, and Mildred Garrett. Alice Richards researched the enormous amount of material we had collected and kept track of what we did use and Phyllis Smith-Flajole typed and retyped the manuscript, mastering the word-processor in the process and producing several re-edited versions. Mildred Garrett did a superb job of the final proofing of the manuscript. The teamwork involved was truly a labor of love.

Jack and Cornelia Addington

INTRODUCTION

How does one love others. Do you find this a challenge at times? Most people do. How many times in thirty-five years in one-to-one counselling we have heard people say, "I want to forgive someone who hurt me years ago, but how? How do you do it?"

Some people are easy to love; others seem almost to defy us to love them. How does one love those who are hard to love?

Jesus advised us to love our enemies, bless those who curse us and do good to them that hate us and even pray for them who have persecuted us. It's a large order isn't it? Everyone who reads this admonition in the Bible wonders, "How do you go about it?"

How can we love enough to get rid of the old hates and resentments? It would seem that we all have a common problem, the temptation to carry along with us a lot of old emotional debris. Long after we think we have left the past behind, we find ourselves reacting emotionally to some situation today that reminds us of a past hurt, some old feeling of rejection that we thought we had overcome long ago. Down deep we know we need to love more, to know that love will overcome these little ugly monsters of the past. But, how? How can we love enough with the hurt and resentment blocking the way?

In this book, we have endeavored to give you love techniques, exercises in loving more, especially designed for those who seem hard to love.

Within each person is a center of love. This is the divine Self, the Christ within. It has always been there, but not always recognized by us. Now is the time to send it forth, like ripples from a pebble cast into the still waters of a lake in ever-widening circles.

On the human level it is easy to love those who love us, but not always easy to love those who resent us. Eventually we come to see that we cannot afford to resent another human soul. It makes us miserable. Eventually it makes us physically ill. It is therefore imperative that we send out those ever-widening circles of love. We must especially send them out to those who have despitefully used us, and might have rejected our love. This is what we mean by "drawing the larger circle."

Start with your nearest and dearest. Draw a circle of love that includes your beloved. It is easy to love this special person. Now draw a larger circle to take in your friends and acquaintances everywhere. Think of your love as flowing out to them, taking them into the circle.

"This is easy," you say. But, how about family problems? that misunderstanding between husband and wife? a generation gap? Is there someone in your office who is hard to love? Do sparks seem to fly when you come together? Can you draw the larger circle and find peace where there was resistance?

Here is a book of "love techniques" that will help you love those who seem hard to love, practical exercises that will help you build a consciousness of love.

Perfect love casts out fear. Perfect love is right within you, ready to be sent forth in ever-widening circles. Learn how to release that perfect love within that *casts out fear.*

Let love go before you to prepare the way. Love will make the crooked places straight. Love will overcome all obstacles and smooth out every rough place in the road. Love is the light on your pathway. Love is the star in the east that leads to the Christ within. *Love is the fulfilling of the law.* Drawing the larger circle is a marvelous way of letting love flower in your life. Learning to love more is the most valuable thing you can ever do. The practical love techniques in this book will help you learn to love more and more and more until your life becomes literally transformed.

When the Dalai Lama, the exiled leader of Tibet and the spiritual guide for the world's millions of Buddhists, left the United States in 1979 after a 46-day tour of the country, he said at a Harvard Divinity School news conference:

"Love is not difficult or complicated to practice. We want happiness as human beings. This (love) is the message."

It is our hope that this book will help the reader discover that love is not difficult or complicated to practice.

Jack and Cornelia Addington

1

DRAWING THE LARGER CIRCLE

He drew a circle that shut me out,
Heretic, rebel, a thing to flout.
But Love and I had the wit to win,
We drew a circle that took him in.
———Edwin Markham

She sat there looking radiant, poised and confident. The alchemy of love had completely transformed her.

I asked her, "Are you as calm as you look?"

Her reply was firm and quick, "I truly am. I have drawn the larger circle. It was difficult; but, once I was able to do it, I changed. I will have no more trouble with this situation. I know that everything is working out right." She smiled a joyful smile that came from her heart.

THE POWER OF LOVE AT WORK

The woman who sat before me was around forty. Mildred (not her real name) was a changed person from the woman I had first known. She and her husband had started a business fifteen years before. They both worked hard and saved and prospered. Five years ago they had decided that she could stay home and be a full-time mother to their three children. Everything seemed to be going along fine.

And then, something happened. The husband announced that he was in love with his secretary. He told her that he did not want a divorce, but preferred the freedom to live with the secretary while keeping up the appearance of liv-ing at home for the sake of the children.

Mildred's reaction to this was indignation, anger, and bit-terness, tinged with a feeling that it could not be true. When her husband failed to put in an appearance at home for several days at a time and she received reports from well-meaning friends, she finally accepted the situation. Her in-dignation turned to hate, mostly directed against the secretary whom she considered to be an impostor, interloper and a husband stealer. She seemed now to be more in love with her husband than ever. She missed him and longed to have him back; but her thoughts would turn black when she thought of the secretary. Mildred had felt betrayed at that point and had come to me for help. I listened as she un-burdened herself. As she talked, I thought, "Love blesses all. Love never fails." I kept thinking of the Apostle Paul's wonderful sermon on love in his letter to the Corinthians.

"Let's have a prayer together," I said. This turned out to be a real cleansing of the mind for her.

We started with love. We knew that there was no power

in conditions, no power in situations; that God is love and love is the only power. We recognized the mighty power of God's love within this entire situation. Love that is *patient and kind...does not insist on its own way...is not irritable or resentful...bears all things...believes all things, hopes all things, endures all things...love never ends.* Affirming these truths aloud we let the cleansing power of love sweep the house clean of the demons of hate and resentment. Little by little, a sense of rejection gave way to the fullness of God's love making her one with life again.

For quite some time after this we sat in the Silence. The ugly little monsters of hate and resentment had slipped away as we forgave each one in the situation and released each to his highest good. You could feel the consciousness of love in the room.

DRAWING THE LARGER CIRCLE

Finally, I broke the Silence by repeating the little poem by Edwin Markham. You see, we did indeed have *the wit to win.* We had drawn a circle *that took him in.* The woman before me looked like a different person. She had become poised and beautiful. There was a radiance about her that was immediately apparent. This technique of drawing the larger circle is most effective in situations involving personal relationships, not only in marriage, but business relationships. Often it is difficult to explain to a person who has been hurt or even grievously wronged that he should forgive the wrongdoer. The subjective tendency is to strike back, to retaliate. This only causes the schism to be widened and the hurt made deeper. At times like this, truth teaches us to act in direct opposite to what we feel. Drawing the larger circle is something that people can understand and apply.

HOW LOVE CHANGED BILL SANDS

I remember meeting the late Bill Sands, a most unusual and interesting man. Bill Sands was a convict. He was in prison in California for a long stretch of time, and was considered incorrigible. He had attacked a fellow prisoner and had been put in solitary confinement. In the course of his stay at San Quentin he had had every kind of punishment, but nothing could make him change his conduct. And then, something happened in that prison. A new warden happened to that prison. When Clinton T. Duffy walked across the threshold at San Quentin a change took place. Warden Duffy was determined that he would bring out the best that was within each man in that enormous prison. The prisoners immediately felt this and they respected him. Warden Duffy was bringing love into an atmosphere of hate and hostility. Love is always received—it may take time for it to be understood, but it is always received for what it is. The turning point in the life of Bill Sands came when he was in solitary and received a visit from the Warden.

Warden Duffy asked him, "Why don't you use your intelligence to work your way out of here?"

This was the first time in years anyone had even associated intelligence with Bill Sands. He was slightly shaken by this. He had not heard anything from anyone on the outside for so long he began to wonder in his mind if he really did want to leave prison. Bill Sands answered him by asking, "Why should I? Nobody cares about me. Nobody."

Duffy looked at him long and steadily and said quietly, "I care."

That did it. SOMEBODY CARED. From that moment on, a gradual change came over Bill Sands. He worked himself up to be a prison clerk. He kept remembering that Warden Duffy cared.

Eventually he was released and made a new life for himself. He wrote two books, one entitled *My Shadow Ran Fast*, and the second, *The Seventh Step*. This book, *The Seventh Step*, tells how Bill Sands founded the extraordinary rehabilitation program through which thousands who would otherwise have spent their lives in prison are free today. Today in prisons all over our country, there are classes in the seven steps to rehabilitation—and a working program conducted outside of the prisons whereby the men who have become rehabilitated may find employment and get a fresh start in life. Someone once asked Bill Sands what was the key idea that caused his program to succeed, and his answer was quick, "love." Here was a former convict who talked about love—and meant it. His seven-step program is built on "love." The words, "I care," spoken by Warden Duffy have been re-echoed thousands of times into a great crescendo, a tremendous thunder of "I care" by thousands of men and women who have become a part of this great program.

LOVE IS THE MISSING INGREDIENT

You know, it occurs to me that none of us achieve emotional maturity until we have learned not only to love our neighbor, to say "I care" and mean it, but have learned to love ourselves. It may surprise you to learn that most of us

5

don't love ourselves; even people who seem to be selfish are often filled with guilt and self-recrimination. Since it is a law of life that the world takes us at our own evaluation, these guilts become blocks that not only keep society from accepting us, but stand in the way of our receiving our good in many ways.

For too long, love has been considered to be something that we *ought* to do. Now, we see that if love does not supplant hate we will destroy ourselves. Hate, resentment and fear are destructive. Love, rightly used, is constructive and it is through love and understanding that a strong and enduring civilization will emerge. Just as Warden Duffy's "I care" struck at the very heart of a hardened convict and affected the lives of thousands, the love that we realize within ourselves and pass on to others will do untold good in helping to bring sanity back to a disturbed world.

LOVE IS THE COMMON DENOMINATOR

Love, being omnipresent, is the common denominator of all of life. As we express love we immediately find that we have something very definite in common with every part of life.

One day I was talking to a well-known lecturer who had made three trips to Europe. Since he spoke only English, I wondered how he managed in some of the countries. He told me that there never was a time when he was at a loss to communicate with others and he believed that it was because he had no motive in his heart but to bring love and truth to others. I mentioned this to a young naval officer who had just returned from the Orient. He agreed wholeheartedly, telling me of the many times he had communicated with Oriental people through an understanding based on love. There are no barriers where love is the bridge.

A recognition of God's love as everywhere present would end wars and petty conflicts. A lack of love in the heart is a sense of separation from God which *is* love. This feeling of separation makes us miserable. The answer to every ill is "where can I love a little bit more?" Sometimes we need to act on love even if it is entirely contrary to the way we are feeling about some certain person or situation. I wish I could picture for you some of the hundreds of times I have seen this work out in the lives of men and women. When love is introduced into a situation, the flood-gates are opened and the alchemy of love begins. Every sort of healing in mind, body and affairs follows after the door of the heart has been opened to God's love.

Your Statement of Love

Beloved, let us love one another: for love is of God: and everyone that loveth is born of God, and knoweth God.[1]

I love the Spirit of God within me. I love the wisdom of God that makes my decisions and motivates my actions. I love the power of God expressing in and through all of life. I love every part of life. I love the little leaf that is green in the spring. I love the brown leaf in the fall. I love the fruit of the trees. I love the food that I take into my body. I love the air that I breathe. I love the sunshine that warms me. I am one with every part of life.

[1] Jn. 4:7.

I love my neighbor and everyone is my neighbor. I see within my neighbor the essence of God that is within me. No antagonistic thought or action can change this love. Love, expressing in and through me, dispels all antagonism.

I love the Lord my God at the center of my being. I love life and life returns my love. Love is all there is and I am part of It. In this awareness I am blessed, uplifted and completely at peace. And so it is.*

*Note: Each chapter ends with a Statement of Love designed to help you recondition your subconscious mind. You will notice that it is written in the first person so that it can be easily applied as you build a consciousness of love. With the exception of ch. 9, these Statements are taken from the authors' book *Your Needs Met* (Marina del Rey, Calif.: DeVorss & Co., 1966). The above Statement of Love will be found on page 11 of that book.

CHAPTER

2

WHAT IS LOVE?

Love is the self-givingness of the Spirit through the desire of Life to express Itself in terms of creation. Love is free from condemnation, even as it is free from fear. Love is a cosmic force whose sweep is irresistible.

Love is the central flame of the universe, nay, the very fire itself. Love is self-givingness through creation, the impartation of the Divine through the human.

—Ernest Holmes
The Science of Mind

Love can heal a sick body; love can make friends out of enemies; love can cause a failing business to prosper. Love could erase all crime, conflict and war from the world.

There is no condition—no matter how fixed and intolerable—which cannot be overcome by love. There is no person, regardless of what depths he has sunk to, who cannot be helped, improved, and lifted up by love.

People since time began have been looking for a panacea, a universal remedy, or a cure-all for their bodily ills and for world problems. There is such a panacea. It is love. Love, properly understood, is the magic key to the kingdom of heaven within. Nothing is impossible to love. It is, in truth, the answer to every human need. *God is love and all things are possible to God.*[1]

LOVE CANNOT BE DEFINED

It is as impossible to define love as it is to define the infinite—for love is infinite.

Love is the highest emotion of feeling that can be experienced. Yet, this is just one tiny facet of love. Love is the energy which created the universe. Love is omnipresent (everywhere present), omnipotent (all powerful), and omniscient (all knowing).

Love is God affirming His creation and calling it good; never condemning; never denying the existence of good. Love continually forgives.

Love is the unlimited power of the universe that transcends every other seeming power. Love is Spirit pouring itself out unstintingly into Its creation and yet never being used up. Love is God expressing as pure feeling through the hearts of all people.

Love is the answer to our every need; irrespective of a seeming obstacle, love is the answer. *God is love and beside Him there is none else.*[2] Love is the one and only power.

To understand love is to understand life. It is only by

[1] 1 Jn. 4:8; Mt. 19:26.
[2] 1 Jn. 4:16; De. 4:39.

misunderstanding love that we misunderstand each other and our relationship to our world.

Love is more than a nice word. It is tremendous energy available at our point of use. Love can be compared to electricity. All of the power of electricity that will ever be used has been here for us, surrounding us all of the time; but we have to understand how to call it forth from the Universal into the specific. The Scripture tells us, *We love because he first loved us.*[3] Infinite love awaits us, but we must particularize it by thinking it, by giving it. We must let love express through us.

SCIENCE HAS PROVED THE POWER OF LOVE

Do you know someone who has a "green thumb"? What is the magic that this person has with plants? It is love. Plants respond to it just as children and animals respond to it. Try loving and blessing one plant and cursing and rejecting another. Although you give the both the same soil, the same food, the same amount of water, the one which you bless will flourish; the one which you curse will wither and die. I personally have seen experiments that prove this a scientific fact.

Jesus cursed the fig tree that through this example he might show the power of mind. Love is the energy of life. Where there is a lack of love, life becomes diminished. We live in proportion to our love.

[3] 1 Jn. 4:19 (RSV).

LOVE OVERCOMES FEAR AND ANXIETY

We must think love, express love, letting go of all resentment. We hate only that which we fear. Fear is the basis of anxiety, worry, and resentment. Envy and covetousness are its children. Fear produces everything that is contrary to love; but, *love casts out fear.*

You and I can express love right where we are. As we make love the basis of our living we are in heaven. Everything in our experience begins to come into harmonious balance. Through love we become poised, moving easily through life without strain. Love is the antidote to strain and stress. Strain and stress are products of fear. Where there is love there can be no fear.

THE GREAT COMMANDMENT IS TO LOVE

Jesus taught the message of love. When a lawyer sought to trap him by asking him which of the commandments was the greatest, he answered at once: *You shall love the Lord your God with all your heart, and with all your soul, and with all your mind. This is the great and first commandment. And the second is like it, You shall love your neighbor as yourself. On these two commandments depend all the law and the prophets.*[4]

Jesus is saying here that love is the answer to everything. If one loved God with all his heart, and soul, and mind, how could he help but love his fellow man? There would be no room for anything else. If one lets love fill his whole being he is letting God live through him into perfect expression.

[4]Mt. 22:37–40 (RSV).

12

Such a one would not know lack or sickness which stem from a sense of separation from love. And so it is said, *The fruit of the Spirit is love — love is the fulfilling of the law.*[5]

"LOVE NEVER GETS TIRED"

A mother and her six-year-old son sat in a crowded waiting room. The little fellow was at the age when he was asking a question a minute. In a period of half an hour he managed to cover almost every subject known to man. To the admiration of everyone in the room, his mother answered each query carefully and patiently.

Inevitably he got around to God. "Where is God? Why is God? What does God do?" etc., etc.

"How does the mother stand it?" those around them wondered.

That question was answered when she answered the little boy's next question.

"Why," he asked, "doesn't God ever get tired and just stop?"

"Because," replied his patient mother, after a moment's thought, "God is love; and love never gets tired."

"LOVE NEVER FAILS"

We hear a lot today about our selfish, decadent society. Don't you believe it. Americans, as a people, are the most loving, generous people in the world.

[5]Gal. 5:22; Rom. 13:10 (RSV).

A New Jersey woman shared this story in one of our widely circulated newspapers:

"When I was a graduate student at Columbia University, I had trouble at first adjusting to the big city with its complex subway system.

"One day I took the wrong subway line, ending up in the Morningside Heights part of Harlem. I knew Columbia was somewhere up over the hill in Morningside Park, but I had heard frightening tales about the park—to avoid it was survival. Yet I had only 50 cents to my name, and I didn't know how else to get where I had to go.

"A woman, seeing my confusion, came up and said, 'No, not the park. Take a taxi.' She pointed one out in spite of my protestations that I couldn't afford it.

"I walked over to the cab and the driver, a native of Harlem, listened to my problem. Then he said simply: 'Hop in—I'll get you there.' Well, he had to charge the initial rate—35¢—but then he turned off his meter and said, 'Okay, miss, now I'm just going to drive around the Columbia area until you spot a familiar section.'

"And that's just what he did, until we found it! The only tip I could give him was a 'thank you'—and a sincere 'God bless you,' for having given me the best gift of all—a deeper sense of brotherhood, a true expression of love."

LOVE IS SHARING

We're still building log cabins for our neighbors. This story of love shared appeared in the Christian Science Monitor:

In November, the Chuck Garrett family lost their house

and belongings in a fire on their homestead west of Fairbanks, Alaska.

A clothing drive was started at the University of Alaska, where the Garretts are employed. Soon it grew into a "Give a Log" drive with university students, instructors, and Fairbanksans contributing to the purchase of the 116 logs needed to build a 24 x 38 foot house.

By the Sunday before Christmas, the road to the homestead had been cleared of snow, and the logs had been hauled in. A house-raising party commenced at 9 A.M., with people of the community joining the activity. The ladies brought desserts and a big Alaska-style stew was provided by University Services. At the end of the day, the young couple and their four children had a home.

ANOTHER GOOD-NEIGHBOR STORY

Wesley Callahan and his wife had worked long and hard to set aside $7,000 for the materials with which he was building his own home. He had the frame well advanced when it caught fire.

Mr. Callahan and his wife were stunned, but they spoke quietly of setting about to save anew and build again.

But the (Annapolis) Evening Capital pictured a scene so vivid and poignant that another sort of flame was ignited: First, came a suggestion of a relief fund for the deserving couple and then the contributions began to flood in. A local savings bank kept the account.

They came generally in very small amounts, but in 10 days they amounted to $9,600.

The picture the paper printed as a sequel shows Mr. Callahan's radiant joy. It was published in full payment of gratitude to all those who reached out a neighbor's hand.

PSEUDO-LOVE IS NOT REAL LOVE

On the human level we are inclined to confuse our terms. Pseudo-love is a sham. On the surface it may seem similar to real love but it is not real. An example of this is "ought-to" love. "Ought-to" signifies a duty or obligation. "I ought to love you—you're my brother, aren't you?" We think we ought to love family members, but do we? "Of course, I love you, you're my wife (husband) aren't you?"

> While he yet talked to the people, behold, his mother and his brethren stood without, desiring to speak with him.
> But he answered and said unto him that told him, "Who is my mother? and who are my brethren?"
> And he stretched forth his hand toward his disciples, and said, "Behold my mother and my brethren!
> For whosoever shall do the will of my Father which is in heaven, the same is my brother, and sister, and mother."[6]

The way we often use the word *love* shows how little many of us know about it. We say, "I love oranges, I love my sports car, I love baseball and I love my wife." We use the same word. Do we mean the same thing? How often we use the word *love* when we mean "I desire; I want to possess; I get gratification from; I exploit; or, I feel guilty about"!

These are all forms of pseudo-love. Pseudo-love is not real love. In this category we find the following types of emotion:

[6]Mt. 12:46–50.

1. Overindulgence of children stemming from selfish pride.
2. Overprotection of one's wife or others out of fear.
3. Possessive feelings and actions akin to jealousy.
4. Self-sacrificing to get attention as a martyr.
5. Sentimental love to gain recognition and acclaim.
6. Idolatrous love marked by excessive adoration and deification of another human being.
7. Love of power, love of possessions, love of money are all forms of self-aggrandizement.

A STATEMENT ON LOVE

The word "love" is so all inclusive, and so intangible as to defy definition.

For our purposes, I like this statement:

> Love is union under the condition of preserving one's integrity, one's individuality. Love is an active power in man; a power which breaks through the walls which separate man from his fellow men, which unites him with others; love makes him overcome the sense of isolation and separateness, yet it permits him to be himself, to retain his integrity. In love the paradox occurs that two beings become one and yet remain two.
>
> —Erich Fromm
> *The Art of Loving*

LOVE IS EVERYWHERE PRESENT

We do not have to make love happen. It has been given to us by God. Love is everywhere present, in and through all of life. It only needs to be recognized and used, and when we understand this we find that there is no obstacle that can stand in its way. As I behold the daily miracle of love at work in the lives of people, I say over and over in awe, "It takes such a little turning to love to bring such a great result."

Love is like a soft, warm light, warming the heart and glowing in every atom of being, radiating out into the farthest corners of our experience.

At one time I did think that we had to generate this love; but, when we think of it as the gift of God, we realize that it is already there, and that we are simply calling it forth from an inexhaustible source when we recognize this. Our point of use is simply a recognition that we are able to bring it into our experience. Then we are able to let God live through us.

YOUR STATEMENT OF LOVE

Yea, I have loved thee with an everlasting love: therefore with lovingkindness have I drawn thee.[7]

God is love, God is infinite and everywhere present in exactly the same degree. How then can I lack love? I dwell in God and God in me and so I am constantly surrounded, enveloped, immersed and completely integrated in infinite love. I can never become separated from this love. It can never be taken away from me for it is my very life, my own true self. Since I know that I have so much love and can

[7]Jer. 31:3.

never lose it, I dare to give it away freely. I send it forth to all the world without reservation and it comes back to me as love in everyone I meet. The love that I feel in my heart is an irresistible magnet drawing love to me from every side. As I consciously dwell in love I am conscious only of love in my life. And so it is.

—*Your Needs Met*, p. 98.

3

LOVE IS FREEDOM

---

*There is no difficulty that enough love will not conquer;
no disease that enough love will not heal; no door that
enough love will not open; no gulf that enough love will
not bridge; no wall that enough love will not throw down;
no sin that enough love will not redeem.*

*It makes no difference how deeply seated may be the
trouble, how hopeless the outlook, how muddled the
tangle, how great the mistake; a sufficient realization of
love will dissolve it all. If only you could love enough you
would be the happiest and most powerful being in the
world.*

—Emmet Fox

Yes, I truly believe that there is *no door that enough love will
not open.* Many people are locked in emotional prisons of
their own making. Others have taken a wrong turn in the
road and find themselves behind prison walls. Ah, but love
can and does open prison doors and in the process provides
a glorious inner freedom even for those within those prison

walls. In my prison ministry I have talked to many inmates who enthusiastically attest to this.

My friend, the late Doug Hooper, told many such true stories in his books. Actually, it was Doug who was responsible for our ever-growing work in the prisons. It happened like this. Back in 1970 he wrote me that he had been listening to my broadcasts and, as a result, had ordered some of my books. He wondered if I had any printed material that I would be willing to send him to use in a class he was currently conducting for a group of inmates at Folsom Prison, California's maximum security prison. In response to his request, I sent the class a number of my books. At this time, Doug Hooper had been conducting this class one day a month entirely on his own. He was a candy salesman whose time was his own and he paid for all of the books he furnished the men out of his own pocket.

Frankly, I was touched at such dedication and wondered, "What else could I send these men?" It came to me in a flash. I had about fifty sets of my ten-lesson Home Study Course together with the Statement of Truth study cards that went with them. This Home Study Course was later to become our best selling book, *The Perfect Power Within You*, but at that time it was neatly packaged, each lesson in its own manila envelope. It was ideal for the purpose and I sent all fifty sets to him.

Frankly, I was not prepared for the enthusiastic response of this group of convicts in California's toughest maximum security prison. Many of them had been on death row and were considered beyond help. I was, therefore, thrilled beyond words to receive letters from these men telling me how much they were getting from my 10-week, 70-day program for a new life.

The dedicated chaplain who sponsored the prison class wrote asking me if they could reprint the Course in the prison print shop for use in the prison. When I agreed, they printed 200 sets and distributed them among the prison population. The next thing I knew, another printing was in process, and we were able to secure copies from them to share with other prisons that had become interested in this successful rehabilitation program. It literally caught on like wildfire and soon classes were starting in many prisons.

During this period I made several trips to Folsom to speak to the men. I found that those who worked with the Course changed completely. Something had happened to those men. I was particularly impressed by the way some of them had become free in their manner of thinking and speaking. Even under prison conditions, the men who attended the classes were actually radiant, their faces open, eyes shining. They were eager to share their spiritual experience, eager to help others find the help they had found. At the conclusion of my talks the men would take turns speaking. They spoke eloquently of the help they had received since they had begun to understand and use the Perfect Power Within. The change in these prison inmates became so noticeable that many were paroled early. The wonderful part of it all was that in a prison noted for its high rate of recidivism, the men who had discovered the power of love within them *did not return to prison.*

Doug continued to conduct the Abundant Living class at Folsom up until he made his transition in 1983. I came to admire this man very much and looked forward to my visits to Folsom. I would fly up to Sacramento and Doug would pick me up at the airport and we would drive the rest of the way to Folsom. On the way Doug would tell me about some of his experiences with the men. They were thrilling stories. I kept telling him he should write a book. Eventually he wrote a syndicated newspaper column. Out of these columns came several best selling books.[1]

Out of all the stories Doug told me I remember two in particular which I have told and retold in my lectures. They illustrate so beautifully the power of love at work.

First, Doug explained to me about Folsom Prison which he called "the end of the line." He said that when a man reached Folsom it meant that everything else had been tried and failed—every kind of therapy the system had to offer. The inmates housed there are generally thought to be hopeless. Apparently, this pessimistic approach only spurred Doug on, as you shall see.

Doug said that in one of his classes he challenged the men to produce a circumstance that could not be changed. A big fellow named Joe stood up, a man who had been in prison for nearly twenty years, much of that time in solitary confinement. I could just picture his belligerent attitude as Doug went on with the story. He stood up in the class and said, "I've got a circumstance that can't be changed by any change of thinking or attitude."

Joe went on to tell the group that he had an early morning job in the mess hall. Every morning he was awakened at four A.M. and escorted to the kitchen by a very surly guard. The guard would come in cursing loudly, rattling his keys, as if he had set out to awaken the whole cell block. Joe hated this man with a passion. He hated him so much that it was making him a nervous wreck. "The only way I can

---

[1]Doug Hooper, *You Are What You Think*, 2 vols. (Hooper Publications, P.O. Box 792, Danville, CA 94526).

change this situation is to hit him over the head, which is exactly what I am going to do someday!" he told the group.

Doug said that he could tell by the way Joe said it that this event was not too far off. He said he told him, "All right, but let's try something else first." And then, Doug really shocked him and the whole group by telling him to feel sorry for the guard. He explained what a miserable, unhappy person that guard must be to act the way he did.

Wow! This was really a revolutionary idea to that group of hard-boiled individuals. I could just picture their mouths hanging open in disbelief as Doug told Joe that the next morning when the guard came around he should say "good morning" to him.

I imagine Doug wondered often during the interim between his visits to Folsom just how this scenario would turn out. No doubt he did some prayer work on it, considering the very happy ending.

When Doug returned for the next class, Joe was there with a big grin on his face. It was the first time Doug had ever seen him smile. Doug was chuckling as he told me the rest of Joe's story. Joe told him: "I lay awake all that night wondering how I was going to say good morning to that S.O.B., but I managed to grunt it out. It stopped him cold! The next morning he (the guard) came in quietly and we grunted good morning to each other. The third morning we started talking and found we had a mutual interest in fishing and hunting. Since then, we have become friends, and he has changed his attitude toward others and is becoming well liked."

Somebody had to change first. Joe changed and the guard changed. "But," Doug commented, "even if the guard hadn't changed, it wouldn't have mattered as far as Joe was concerned. The situation had lost its power to hurt him the minute he changed his mind about it! In fact, Joe changed so completely after this incident that he was released much sooner than he had previously dared to hope." Later he wrote Doug that it had given him such a wonderful feeling to know that he had the power within himself to handle any situation that might come along, simply by controlling his thoughts and his attitudes. Love had set him free. The guard *had drawn a circle that shut him out, but love and Joe had the wit to win. They drew a circle that took him in!*

Somebody had to make the first move. Joe made it. And when love and understanding came into the picture the walls of hate and distrust melted. Love brought a new feeling of freedom into Folsom Prison that ultimately brought about Joe's release.

THE POWER OF LOVE IS TRULY AWESOME

Doug was full of stories. The drive from Sacramento to Folsom never seemed long enough. I'll never forget the day he told me about Norman. It rained hard all the way. The sky was dark and foreboding but Doug fairly glowed as he told me this story. He said that any doubts he ever had concerning the power of love were dispelled during a class he conducted for about 75 prisoners at San Quentin Prison. He was trying to impress these 75 hard-boiled men that love was more powerful than hate. Not one agreed with him. One of the men, a man named Norman, gave him the most vehement argument.

Norman had been incarcerated for three years. His wife and two children lived in Seattle and he had not heard from her all during that time. During this period Norman had let his hatred and resentment for her fester. In fact, he spent most of his waking moments plotting how he would murder her when he got out of prison. When he heard Doug say that love was so powerful that it transcends time and space he really became aroused.

"If what you say is true," he growled, "you should be able to show me how to get a letter from my wife. I haven't heard from her since I've been here."

I could just picture it all. The other men silent, taking it all in. Norman with a sarcastic grin on his face, sure that he had the teacher stumped this time.

But Doug, as usual, was equal to the challenge because he really believed that the spiritual laws he was teaching these men were infallible when put into practice.

"Let me ask you one question first," he said. "Was there ever a time when you and your wife were happy and in love with each other?"

Norman had to admit that there was. He said that the first few years were fine. Their family was a very happy one.

"All right," Doug said, "if you will do exactly as I say I believe that you will receive a letter from her. For the next two weeks your every thought must be concentrated upon those happy times. Whenever you think of your wife and children it must be with thoughts of love. Refuse to entertain any thoughts of hatred or revenge."

This must have seemed like a large order to Norman, but he agreed to try the experiment. Two weeks later when Doug returned for the next class, he said he hardly recognized Norman. Whereas before his face had registered hate, now he looked peaceful and his perpetual frown had disappeared. He had a letter in his hand. He tried to read it to the group but became so emotional that he couldn't continue. He asked Doug to read it for him. Doug said that he did with difficulty. When he finished there wasn't a dry eye in the room. Doug never forgot that letter and I, too, remember it almost word for word as Doug quoted it to me:

> Dear Norman:
> I hope you will forgive me for not writing for so long. A strange thing happened a few days ago. I remembered all the happy times we had together, and I was overwhelmed by a feeling of love for you. The children and I want you back and we are waiting for you.

LOVE DOES OPEN PRISON DOORS

The late Starr Daily wrote the book *Love Can Open Prison Doors*. Love did open prison doors for Starr Daily and after that he spent the rest of his life dedicating himself to bringing the message of love to people all over the world. Through telling his own experience, he helped so many people that eventually all of his old suffering must have seemed to him more than worthwhile.

Starr Daily wrote of having been a habitual criminal. After he had re-entered prison for the third time, and three times attempted escape, the plot was discovered and he was sentenced to the dungeon. For fifteen days he was in "the hole" as it is called in some prisons. Finally he collapsed. His writings tell, in his own words, a very thrilling account of what happened to him then. I would call it, briefly, a complete spiritual rebirth. In his book he tells how he was released from the dungeon, how he was beaten for his prison offenses and how in the very midst of his beating he felt a great feeling of compassion for his tormentors whom formerly he had hated so bitterly. He began to love them and silently bless them. So great is the power of love that they immediately stopped beating him. They couldn't continue when he loved them. The wives of the prison officials became concerned about him and when he was returned to his cell sent him small comforts and began to take an interest in his welfare. He said that the prison doors swung open five years in advance of the time set for his release. Why? Because love filled his heart.

I myself witnessed an almost parallel situation when I went before a judge, in the capacity of a minister, with a young man who had enough against him to send him up for life. He had a record a mile long—car theft, bank robbery, bad checks. He had been sent up several times and had escaped twice. I met him in the line after church after I had given a sermon on the power of love. Little did I know the effect my talk was to have on this man. The following day he turned himself in to the federal authorities. At his request I went to the jail to see him. It was then that I learned that this young man had been running from the authorities for three years.

I went to see the federal district attorney who showed me the fellow's record consisting of four pages' single-spaced typing. The federal district attorney said, "We're going to go for the maximum on this, all we can get, and he should get life." He said a lot would depend on the recommendation of the probation officer.

I then went to see the probation officer who also had a copy of the record. He told me I was wasting my time. The probation officer told me that nothing could save him. He said the judge would "throw the book at him."

Remember, this young man had offered himself up to the authorities because love had come into his heart. He was a changed person. He went before the judge without even legal counsel. He gave such an inspired plea that the judge, a judge of the federal court, actually apologized to him, saying: "I've got to give you some kind of sentence considering your bad record. How would it be if I sent you to McNeil's Island for a year with two months off for good behavior?" The prosecuting attorney and the probation officer were astounded and even I who lived with miracles was dumbfounded. Love had won another case.

Your Statement of Love

I will show you a still more excellent way.[2]

Love walks in and opens the door when all else fails. There is no problem on earth that love cannot heal.

Love is the answer to my every need. Love guides me into paths of right-use-ness. Love heals antagonism and dispels hatred. I let love correct any misunderstandings in my life. I let love go before me and prepare the way.

I trust my dear ones to omnipresent love right where they are. I know that they are safe and divinely protected because love never fails.

I am centered in love. Right where I am is all the love that there is. Love opens the door to divine right action in my life. Love heals me. Love corrects me and cleanses my heart. Love is a more excellent way to a perfect experience. The love of God is my eternal blessing. And so it is.

—*Your Needs Met*, p. 94.

[2]1 Cor. 12:31 (RSV).

CHAPTER

4

PERFECT LOVE CASTS OUT FEAR

---

*God is love, and he who abides in love abides in
God...There is no fear in love, but perfect love casts
out fear.*[1]

God is love the Bible tells us. Therefore, when we love we
partake of the nature of God. What does that mean? If God
is love, and you are feeling love, being love, letting love express through you, even for one moment, in that one moment you are experiencing your godhood. And that's as
close to God as you're ever going to get. You just can't get
any closer. God lives in and through you as love. Therefore,
God is love expressed in our lives.

If man is the image and likeness of God, as the Bible
assures us he is, then man is God as he portrays God to be.
Each in his own way. When you love you are letting God
be expressed in all His glory in this life. Love is a state of consciousness, and when we are aware of love, expressing it, we
are living the Spirit.

[1] Jn. 4:16, 18 (RSV).

HOW DOES PERFECT LOVE CAST OUT FEAR?

For years I struggled with this thought: *Perfect love casts out fear*. I kept thinking, "That's great, that's wonderful, but where is perfect love?" And then it came to me—perfect love is God's love, not my human love, but the love of God that I am able to express through me. Spiritual love has to be true love, God's love, or *perfect love*. *Perfect love* is right within you, and when you consciously feel love and subconsciously feel love, it is the unity of the inner and the outer, the thinking-feeling nature unified at one time.

When the conscious and subconscious unite in perfect harmony in the expression of love, that is perfect love. We can only think one thought at a time. When we are thinking, consciously thinking, "I love," and nothing in us resists this love, then you have *perfect love*.

There is no place for fear in this conscious awareness of love. There is no place for hate.

Sometimes people talk love with their lips. But down deep they are indifferent to it. It is just a matter of giving lip service to love. But, when love is total, when it is within and without, on the lips and in the heart, there is *perfect love*. This is the kind of love that casts out fear, casts out hate, resentment, jealousy, envy and indifference.

LOVE IS PROTECTION

Love not only casts out fear but wraps the one who loves in an impervious mantle of protection. Hundreds of true stories prove this to be a fact.

Back in 1960 I heard Marcus Bach tell this story to Doug Lowe during an interview on the Night Owl Program. Dur-

31

ing the time that Marcus Bach was doing research for his book on the religions of the world he spent some time in Haiti interviewing a white doctor there regarding voodooism and the religious ceremonies of Haiti. Bach said that one night he and the doctor were walking along a street in Haiti followed closely by a group of young Haitian blacks, who were taunting them, yelling ugly names and jeers at them. As the group kept getting closer and closer the doctor suggested they just walk along and ignore them. Finally the doctor turned and to the surprise of Bach spoke to them in faultless Creole, their own language. He said, "Why do you taunt us for being white? Can I help it if the Creator ran out of color before he made me?" The blacks were suddenly silent, overcome by the love in the man's voice. One of them fell to his knees in prayer. Marcus Bach continued, "I don't want to overdramatize this story but they were powerful men. One of them was over six feet four inches tall."

Love had triumphed. Love not only overcomes fear but casts out hate. Love begets love.

In his powerful book *The Ways and Power of Love*, Pitirim A. Sorokin begins the Preface with these words:

> Blessed are the meek: for they shall inherit the earth. Blessed are the merciful: for they shall obtain mercy. Blessed are the peacemakers; for they shall be called the children of God. —Jesus

> In 1918 I was hunted from pillar to post by the Russian Communist Government. At last I was imprisoned and condemned to death. Daily, during six weeks, I expected to be shot, and witnessed the shooting of my friends and fellow prisoners. During the subsequent four years of my stay in Communist Russia I underwent other painful experiences

and observed, to the heartbreaking point, endless horrors of human bestiality, death, and destruction. Exactly in these conditions I jotted down in my diary the following "observations of a cold intellect and plaintive murmurs of a saddened heart.":

Whatever may happen in the future, I know that I have learned three things which will remain forever convictions of my heart as well as my mind. Life, even the hardest life, is the most beautiful, wonderful, and miraculous treasure in the world. Fulfillment of duty is another marvelous thing making life happy. This is my second conviction. And my third is that cruelty, hatred, violence, and injustice never can and never will be able to create a mental, moral, or material millennium. The only way toward it is the royal road of all-giving creative love, not only preached but consistently practiced.[2]

When he wrote *The Ways and Power of Love* thirty-five years had passed since his imprisonment in Russia, years filled with more tragic events as well as scientific studies which reenforced his belief in the power of love and led him to write:

Now more than ever before I believe the following truths, which are fully confirmed by our experimental studies: Hate begets hate, violence engenders violence, hypocrisy is answered by hypocrisy, war generates war, and love creates love.

Page after page of his book is filled with examples of how love overcomes fear and hatred.

[2]Pitirim A. Sorokin, *The Ways and Power of Love* (Boston: Beacon Press, 1954).

I particularly enjoyed the story of Toyohiko Kagawa who *has so much security inside that he can afford to go without any outside.* Alone in his tiny room on the Shinkawa slums, he was awakened one night by a drunk or half-drunk gangster, with sword uplifted. As I picture this scene, I wonder if you or I would be able to face the situation fearlessly. Love overcame fear for Kagawa who got to his knees and bowed his head in prayer as he awaited the blow. Instead the man said to him, "Kagawa, do you love me?" Kagawa answered, "Yes, I do." Then the man said, "Here's a present," and he left Kagawa his sword.

Sorokin told this story of how love protected an elderly lady from a burglar:

> A friend of mine, an elderly Quaker lady, entered her Paris hotel room to find a burglar rifling her bureau drawers where she had considerable jewelry and money. He had a gun which he brandished. She talked to him quietly, told him to go right ahead and help himself to anything she had, as obviously he needed it more than she did if he had to be stealing it. She even told him some places to look where there were valuables he had overlooked. Suddenly the man let out a low cry...and ran from the room taking nothing. The next day she received a letter from him in which he said, "I'm not afraid of hate. But you showed love and kindness. It disarmed me."

It is said that animals can smell fear in human beings and that if you overcome your fear they will never hurt you. Two stories told by Pitirim Sorokin bear this out.

When wolves were needed for a Hollywood movie, Larry Trimble offered to train twenty of them. How would you like to sleep with twenty wild wolves? That is exactly what this man did. He let the wolves loose in a twenty-acre stockade. Then he left pieces of meat out in the open and curled up in his sleeping bag in the same area. He was completely defenseless but confident. Before long the wolves were eating out of his hand and sleeping within a few yards of him.

Helen Keller saw things through her finger tips. She desired to "see" a lion and although she was warned not to go into the lion's cage, she insisted on doing so. Just imagine a person who could not see or hear walking fearlessly into a lion's cage! Helen Keller walked into the lion's cage without fear, her heart filled with love for the lion. Inquiringly, she knelt before the surprised lion which offered no resistance to her touch. As she explored the lion's muscles, mane, paws, tail, etc., it roared. Of course, Helen did not hear the roar. The lion sensing her love and lack of fear made no effort to stop her. Again perfect love had cast out fear.

LOVE DISPELS THE DARKNESS

There is an old saying, "It is better to light one candle than to curse the darkness." When we tell someone "I love you," when we spread love, even the little that each one is able to do, we are lighting a candle in the darkness and our light shines a long way.

A friend of mine has an old and well-worn Bible belonging to his father who was a minister. In it I found on the flyleaf this little verse:

> I am only one,
> But still, I am one.
> I cannot do everything,

But still, I can do something.
And because I cannot do everything,
I will not refuse to do the something
    that I can do.

Sometimes we feel futile about the something we can do, but when it comes to love we must never feel that way, for a little love will start a chain of love that will reach around the world. We see this so clearly in our work with the prisons. Love multiplies like seeds in a flower garden. Men and women are turning their lives around because somebody cares and, often for the first time in their lives, they feel they are loved. Here is a poem that was written by one of the young women at a women's prison. It was written by a person who had blossomed when she felt loved.

On life's busy thoroughfare,
    We meet with angels unaware,
So please make us kind and wise,
    So we may always recognize,
The blessings that are ours to take,
    The friendships that are ours to make
If we but open our heart's door wide
    To let the sunshine of life inside.

LOVE BEGETS LOVE

A woman called my office one day and told me that she had been married for 27 years, but that she and her husband had never known a day of rapport with each other. There was something lacking. She had prayed over this but there was still that gap in their relationship. It occurred to me that

36

there had probably never been any love exchanged between them. Somebody had to make the first move. So I suggested to her that she put up cards in each room that said in large letters I LOVE YOU.

This she did and when her husband came home that evening he began to smile. They started to talk and the barriers between them began to melt. There was a different feeling in the atmosphere. The next day she called to tell us, "Our lives have changed! We have a completely different life. Now we are able to say, back and forth, 'I love you!' and mean it."

You can walk up to a total stranger and say, "I love you." It's really very easy. You just say it in your heart.

AN EXPERIMENT IN LOVE

One time when I was practicing law, I made an experiment. I was on my way to the court house, a walk of about a mile from my office. That day, as I was walking along, I decided that in my heart I would greet every person, without smiling—I made it a point to keep an immobile face—that in my heart I would say to each person, "I love you." It was the most amazing experience. People turned around to smile and say "Good morning." They could feel that "I love you." Since then I have done this many times. Try it for yourself; it will make you feel wonderful and, of course, that feeling will be shared by everyone you meet.

Let love be your dominant thought, your overriding feeling. Ask yourself in everything you do, "Is this the loving thing to do? Is this the loving answer? Am I letting God's love live through me as I take this step?" As you drive your car, ask yourself, "Is love driving my car?" When people snarl at you in traffic, possibly shaking their fist at you, love them. Just love them. Love them and forgive them. When you feel unloving, forgive yourself immediately. You can get off the track every now and then. Something may trip you up, tempting you to feel resentment. When this happens, affirm quickly, "I love him. I do not like what he does, but I love him. I refuse to become entangled in his web of anxiety, fear and hate. I love him!"

LOVE MEETS EVERY CHALLENGE

Booker T. Washington once said, "I'll never let any man drag me down to the point of where I hate him." And that's what we all have to remember. When we are tempted to resent someone, it makes no difference what he may have done, that's his problem, not our problem. We can help him and help ourselves by loving him. Love is truly the answer to every need. Love is the answer to every problem, to every challenge. It makes no difference what the problem is.

Love can heal a sick body. People say to me, "How can I pray for another?" It's really very simple. Sit down and start surrounding the person you are thinking of with love. Love him. Love her. Feel this love through your whole being. Then right thoughts and right words and right ideas will come to you. The real work is done when you start loving.

Albert Cliffe tells a story of the healing power of love that I have never forgotten. I have passed it on to many people.[3] Cliffe said that a man crippled with a form of arthritis came to visit him one day. The man was on crutches, barely able

[3]Albert E. Cliffe, *Lessons in Successful Living*, (Englewood Cliffs, N.J.: Prentice-Hall, 1950).

to get around. Cliffe asked him how this condition had begun and was told that the condition had first shown up about six years previously. At that time he and his brother were partners but they had a falling out. They parted in anger and the families refused to speak to each other. It came out as they talked that the man had developed hate toward his brother and as his hate grew so did his sickness. Now crippled, he wanted God to help him.

Cliffe showed him the evil of his ways and told him that he must practice complete forgiveness of that wrong even if it were true, as he said, that his brother had robbed him. He must ask forgiveness of his brother and tell God that he wanted to be forgiven for hating his brother. Together they prayed over this and the man was able to find complete forgiveness in his heart for his brother. He dictated a letter to his brother on the spot and sent it by special messenger. At that point Dr. Cliffe said that a surprising thing happened. *The man arose to go and suddenly walked across the room, put his hat and coat on, and thanked Dr. Cliffe.* Then Dr. Cliffe asked, "What about your two crutches over there?" He had not realized that for the first time in years he did not need the crutches. He never needed them again. Love had triumphed. Love, the healing power within each one of us, can perform the miracle once we unify with it.

LOVE IS A COMMANDMENT

Jesus thought it so important he made it a commandment. *I give you a new commandment,* he said: *Love one another.*[4]

And isn't that the way it is? We have to continually com-

[4]Jn. 13:34.

mand ourselves to love. Otherwise, we become indifferent, isolated. It doesn't mean we go down the street saying, "O.K., I'm not going to bother a soul. I'm not going to get in anybody's hair. I am not going to cause anybody any trouble. I am just going to walk down the street and encase myself in a little protective shell, and anybody who comes within my orbit is going to find he is dealing with the wrong person. I am not going to hurt anybody, but I'm not going to do anything for anybody either." That's indifference, and indifference is almost worse than hate. At least when you hate you're involved and interested in another person. But when you are indifferent you aren't thinking at all. You are rejecting life.

When you love you are using the great power, the only power, the power of love. I have had, in my life, problems that seemed to me insurmountable, and I would turn to the Father within and say, "God, what do we do now?" And then it would come through like a great pounding surge from within: "Love. Love and understand."

Sometimes I have been still for nearly a whole day, just thinking these thoughts: "I love this person. I understand this person. I love," until I was able to erase all of the feeling of resistance in my own consciousness.

LOVE IS CONTAGIOUS

You see, the thing about love is that it is contagious. Why? You've heard the song "Love Is a Many Splendored Thing." Love *is* a many-splendored thing. It covers every area of living. There is an infinite variety of facets in love.

When we turn to love and think and feel love, love begets

love. That was the great discovery of the Buddha, that good begets good, and love begets love. Love is first cause. Love goes before us to prepare the way. Love goes before us to make the crooked places straight. Love goes before us to part the waters. Love is creative. Love is intuitive. Love is imaginative. When we turn to love we have answers we never dreamed of.

The Bible says, *We love, because he first loved us.*[5] God's love is everywhere present. God loves you first. Therefore, when you start loving God, you don't have to make God be there. Love is already waiting for you. When you start loving God, you start loving love, and you let love be expressed in your life.

God has such wondrous ways of working everything out for us. Next time you feel that you are in a tight spot and things don't seem to be going right, try turning to the presence of love, right within you, God within you, and think to yourself, "I love you, I love you, I love you." Turn within and think, "God, how I love You. How I love every part of Your wonderful life." And as you let your heart become wrapped in love, you will feel the love that is beyond all understanding, all definition, that great inward feeling that comes when God comes through the door that you have now opened by loving.

Your Statement of Love

Owe no one anything, except to love one another; for he who loves his neighbor has fulfilled the law.[6]

[5]1 Jn. 4:19 (RSV).
[6]Rom. 13:8 (RSV).

The illimitable love of God expressing in and through me directs me, protects me, and fulfills all of the desires of my life. I know no feeling of separation from any living soul for we are all one as the love of God works in and through His perfect creation. I send my love out to all of the world and it returns to me from everyone I contact. In this way I attune myself with God's wonderful storehouse of infinite love and I am blessed, protected, and prospered in everything that I do. I am eternally grateful that I am a divine expression of God's perfect love and that this love is the motivating power of my life.

I love the Lord, my God, with all my heart, and with all my soul, and with all my mind; and my neighbor as myself. And thus God's perfect law is fulfilled through me. And so it is.

—*Your Needs Met*, p. 95.

5

THE LOVE WE GIVE AWAY WE KEEP

A bell is not a bell till you ring it.
A song is not a song till you sing it.
Love was not put in your heart to stay.
Love is not love till you give it away.
　　　　　—Oscar Hammerstein II (1895–1960)

I have long been an admirer of the late Oscar Hammerstein II. Best known for the lyrics of *South Pacific*, *Oklahoma*, *Carousel* and other musicals, he was a gentle person, quiet, unassuming and loving. He may not have liked all people but he respected them and always had time to help someone.

We are apt to think that the words and the music for musicals are written simultaneously. This was not the case with Oscar Hammerstein. He wrote the words arranged as poetry. In other words, he was a modern-day poet, and a good one. His words were heard and sung by millions of people.

A New York taxi driver who often drove him, when asked what he thought of Hammerstein, replied, "He was a healing sort of a guy." I think that says a lot. A man who worked with him on one of the musicals said, "Oscar really believed that love conquers all, that virtue triumphs, that dreams do come true." When someone accused Hammerstein of being a sentimentalist, his answer was, "There's nothing wrong with sentiment. The things people are sentimental about are the fundamental things of life. I don't deny the ugly and the tragic, but somebody has to keep saying that life's pretty wonderful, too, because it's true. I guess I just can't write anything without hope in it."

I say, thank God for the Oscar Hammersteins of this world! Thank God for people who do not succumb to the idea that being realistic means dwelling continuously on the negative, the destructive and the sordid side of life, but hold that beauty, love and joy are expressive of man's true nature. As Oscar Hammerstein wrote for *South Pacific*:

> You've got to be taught to be afraid
> Of people whose eyes are oddly made
> And people whose skin is a different shade.
> You've got to be taught to be afraid.

Mary Martin visited him in the hospital the day before he departed this life experience. He handed her a note that he had scribbled during the day. These were his last written words:

> A bell is not a bell till you ring it.
> A song is not a song till you sing it.
> Love was not put in your heart to stay.
> Love is not love till you give it away.

What a great man! Perhaps these last words explain why his thoughts touched and moved the hearts of millions of people throughout the world.

SURROUNDED BY A CIRCLE OF LOVE

We all want to be loved; we want to feel that those we love will love us in return. Sometimes, we pour our love out freely to someone near us and when it does not come back in the same measure we give it, we are hurt. We are apt to feel that life has been unfair. Very often we are afraid to give love after that, lest we be hurt again. To understand impersonal love is sometimes the hardest lesson of all. It takes a long time to understand that love always returns, but not always from some certain designated personality whom we expected to love us. When we measure love we are almost sure to be disappointed. As long as we continue to give people the power to hurt us, we are going to go on suffering. We cannot understand why people act the way they do and so we are inclined to blame ourselves.

"Where have I failed? Why did this happen to me? I trusted this person, I loved this person. How can someone I loved so much treat me this way?" we ask ourselves.

At the human level there are no answers. For some strange reason, people who *oppose themselves*, as Paul, the apostle, so neatly put it, have a great need to shift the blame for their own irritation upon someone else. Paradoxically, the whipping boy is generally someone close to them, one who has given special love and attention, such as a mother, wife, or close friend. An unhappy person may lash out at another without provocation. To understand and forgive

45

not only takes spiritual growth but requires patience, understanding and compassion.

At that crucial moment when we are tempted to accept the hurt, we must put on the armor of love. Love disarms all aggressors and turns aside the barbed arrows. We need not be the target for they were not really meant for us. Quickly, we remind ourselves, "I am surrounded by a circle of love. Human hatred cannot penetrate this circle." Then, silently address the troubled person, "I love you. I understand you. I forgive you."

Again we have drawn the larger circle.

HOW DO WE REACT, WITH LOVE OR HATE?

A woman who lives in Minneapolis wrote us recently of a situation where she felt she was unjustly treated. I will let her tell the story.

What brings about unhappy and unsuccessful experiences in our lives when we are doing our utmost to be kind, loving, honest with others?

I have in mind a recent experience. I took a job for two and one-half days a week in a medical office. After the first week they wanted me on a four-day basis. I had the "know-how" from 20 years' previous experience, so I needed very little supervision in doing the medical insurance claims billing.

In putting the old material in each patient's new chart it was necessary to remove old staples and restaple. I was working along with my heart singing because I knew I was doing a fine job when suddenly I heard a voice that did not even sound like the bookkeeper, whose desk was right at my elbow, saying so harshly: "Look what you are doing." I was so shocked that I could not even speak. She went on in almost a violent manner, "We've been seeing these staples and have been wondering if you are throwing them on the floor in bunches." She continued, "Doctor just put in this new linoleum and I want to keep it nice for him, so you just get a wet Kleenex and clean them up."

Now I am not supersensitive because I have worked in offices a long time and gotten along well, but what she said and in the manner she said it, crushed me. I told her later when I resigned, "Why didn't you just ask me where all the staples were coming from? I could have discussed it with you and we could have worked it out satisfactorily." No one cautioned me about preserving the floor, and no one really cared a hang about preserving me either. I finally came out of my shock long enough to say, "The staples come from removing old materials from the chart and some are bound to break off and fall on my desk and possibly on the floor." I did clean up the floor before I went home. In resigning I told the bookkeeper, "I would be afraid to make a mistake in the future if you could blow up so about a few staples."

I am most orderly in my home, my work, what I say to people, and in controlling my thoughts and behavior. But, I continually have this kind of treatment from family and outsiders. And it always comes as a complete shock. What would cause anyone to use such treatment of someone they needed and wanted to stay with them? She had told many people, "We have a very good insurance secretary now, and we want her to stay with us."

But I did not want to work elbow to elbow with someone like that. What would the future bring if something more serious were to arise?

This letter is a very good example of how people punish themselves by reacting to something outside of themselves.

It is the same old story: *It is not what is done to us that matters, but how do we react?* One cannot control the words or the thoughts of another, but one *can* control his own thoughts and responses.

It all reminds me of a story that is told about Gautama the Buddha. One time he entered a village and was stopped by a man who began to curse and malign him. Finally the man wore himself out. When he had finished, the Buddha asked him a question: "If a person offered you a gift and you did not accept it, to whom does the gift belong?"

The man answered, "To the person who tried to give it to you."

The Buddha then replied, "I do not accept your words and your thoughts, therefore they still belong to you, not to me." He walked away from the man.

Now, the Buddha could have retaliated in any number of ways, ways which would have caused him suffering and caused him to lose his poise, but he would only have hurt himself. Since he did not accept what the man said, it did not become his experience.

It is evident that the writer of the letter wanted to retaliate against the bookkeeper, to get even for the hurt inflicted. The only person she could hurt was herself. She lost a good job. She could have ignored the whole thing and cleaned up the staples. She could have met the situation with love and understanding and become a peacemaker.

We are the only ones who have control over our emotions. When we let an immature person control us, we descend to that person's level. The mature person rises above the emotional impact of the situation and keeps his cool. When we know who we really are we do not need to struggle with the cruel accusations of someone who may be trying to get at us.

Had this woman prayed for the irate bookkeeper, blessing and forgiving her, she would no doubt still have her good job and quite probably would have had an apology from her fellow worker and gained a close friend.

I once had just such a situation in my own life. When I blessed this very difficult personality in my office, she came to me and asked me where she could find some of what I had. With great joy, I shared my Truth literature with her. I had let my light shine and we were both richer for the experience. It turned out to be a blessing rather than a curse.

It was then that I began to understand what Jesus meant when he said *he who loses his life shall find it.* When we have reached the point where another's unkind, spiteful remarks can no longer wound us, we have found the true Self. We have only lost the personality self that rises and falls by outer applause and sinks to defeat in the heat of criticism. When we lose our bondage to ego we discover our spiritual identity, and loss is gain.

We are secure forever in the knowledge of unchanging love. Nothing from without can hurt us unless we let it. When we hold fast to love we can say, *Father, forgive them for they know not what they do,*[1] and really mean it.

People spend their lives trying to get love when the only love we can ever know is the love we experience within, the love that we give to others. When we become still and pour out the love of God we hear the Voice within reassuring us,

---

[1] Lk. 23:34 (RSV).

49

Be still and know that I am God [within you]; I will never fail you nor forsake you.[2]

Thus it behooves us, if we would be the children of God, to *love our enemies, bless them that curse us, do good to them that hate us, and pray for them which despitefully use us, and persecute us.*[3]

Jesus said, *It is easy to love those who love you.* The challenge is to love our enemies. The pure in heart see only love. If we accept hate and derision, then we have allowed ourselves to become separated from the divine center within. When we succumb to false accusations and fight back we put ourselves on the level of the aggressor and allow the "enemy" to win. Temporarily, we have lost our right to be called one of the children of God, the right of sonship with the Father which is all-love. Then we must *pass out of love's threshing floor, into the seasonless world where you shall laugh, but not all of your laughter, and weep, but not all of your tears.*[4] To me, Gibran meant by this that we must experience this particular point of spiritual growth again and again until we have overcome it at last and risen above the temptation to fight back. The ultimate growth is to know that love is all-power. Hate has no power over us when we understand this.

To love is not to count the cost but to give freely with no strings attached. Impersonal love does not say, "I will love you if you will love me in return," but loves all freely and asks for no reward or recognition. Even if our love is refused we are richer for having loved.

[2]Ps. 46:10 (RSV); Heb. 13:5 (RSV).
[3]Mt. 5:44 (RSV).
[4]Kahlil Gibran, *The Prophet*, (New York: Alfred A. Knopf, 1936).

Your Statement of Love

Great peace have they which love thy law; and nothing shall offend them.[5]

Nothing offends me for I am grounded in love. God is my protection, I shall not fear. My conscious awareness of love is a protection to myself and those who know me.

Love is the only power. Only love goes from me and only love returns to me. There is nothing to fear. Love heals antagonism. Love nullifies resentment. Love guards and protects. I dwell peacefully in love, knowing constant protection. Love welds me together with all mankind. Never again need I feel lonely or afraid. Divine love at the center of my being is my freedom from sin and mistake. Since love surrounds me at all times, there is nothing to resent.

I trust perfect love at the center of my being. And so it is.

— *Your Needs Met*, p. 131.

[5]Ps. 119:165.

6

LOVE IS THE HEALER
OF MIND AND BODY

For without love we lose the will to live. Our mental and physical vitality is impaired, our resistance is lowered, and we succumb to illnesses that often prove fatal. We may escape actual death, but what remains is a meager and barren existence, emotionally so impoverished that we can only be half alive.

—Smiley Blanton, M.D.
Love or Perish

Remember the old song—*What the World Needs Now Is Love, Sweet Love?* How true, how true! What the world needs today is love and plenty of it. Everywhere we turn today there are many evidences of hate, resentment, jealousy and fear; emotions that destroy, emotions that are just the opposite of love.

Fortunately, more and more people are discovering the power of love to heal and restore human beings.

DOCTORS ARE FINDING LOVE IS THE BEST MEDICINE

Doctors at the Menninger Clinic at Topeka, Kansas, have for some years prescribed "TLC" on their charts. The nurses know that this means *Tender, Loving Care*. So widespread has the meaning of TLC become that you will find it listed in many modern dictionaries.

Many doctors are proving that TLC is most effective in healing people of all ages. It has been found that elderly people considered to be senile make rapid improvement when love is introduced into their therapy. Recently a program has been introduced whereby little animals, kittens and puppies are brought into homes for the elderly so that they may stroke them and cuddle them. It has been found that the patients brighten and become more and more alert as this love therapy progresses.

At the Neonatal Intensive Care Unit at the University of Connecticut Health Center the "Cuddlers Program" was started back in 1980. The results speak for themselves. I think this article from the *San Diego Union* will interest you:

CUDDLING A TINY PACKAGE BACK TO HEALTH

Anne Hartman gently rocks the tiny 2-pound baby with its few tufts of hair and hands the size of quarters.

"This is therapy for me as well as him" says Hartman, whose own offspring are fully grown.

In the Neonatal Intensive Care Unit, treatment isn't limited to monitoring the heart rates, pulses and breathing of the infants struggling for survival in thier isolettes.

53

To combat special developmental problems, volunteer "cuddlers" hope to speed healing and compensate for the lack of a warm, nurturing home environment by holding, feeding, stroking and soothingly talking to babies whose parents cannot be with them all the time.

Patricia Thurston, the nurse-coordinator of the program at the University of Connecticut Health Center, said the project was organized in 1980 when a premature baby girl rejected food after intestinal surgery.

"We realized the baby was associating eating with pain, and turned her head away when anyone approached her," she said. "While a child development specialist recommended intensive doses of love and handling, the nursing staff didn't have that much time to spend with a single baby.

"That's when the Cuddlers Program started, with volunteers holding and feeding the baby who started associating her bottle with positive feelings."

That infant is now a healthy 5-year-old. Her response inspired the staff to expand the program to other infants, the premature and those recuperating from surgery.

"It's very important they receive some of the same stimulation and handling as a normal infant," said occupational therapist Alisa Palmeri. "Families can't always provide it, particularly when they live far away."

"We see these experiences as essential," she said. "The cuddlers provide the babies with a consistent parent surrogate."

The infants the cuddlers lavish affection upon range in weight from 1 pound, 2 ounces, to normal-size newborns recuperating from operations. Many are irritable from blood tests and other uncomfortable procedures.

"They sleep for longer periods than normal infants and are less receptive to the sight and sound stimulation necessary for normal growth," said Elaine Geary, the other coordinator.

LOVE WORKS MIRACLES

An infant in Temple, Texas, was considered to be a vegetable. He was placed in a nursing home which cared primarily for disabled veterans. Weldon, the illegitimate son of an American GI and a Korean woman, had been born with severe physical defects. After his mother gave him up he had been cared for in the Army hospitals in Korea, in Hawaii and finally in Fort Hood, Texas.

At two months, Weldon had undergone open heart surgery. But that was not all. He suffered from more than a dozen health disorders including neurological defects and chronic pneumonia. He was diagnosed as being blind, deaf and mute. He was unable even to swallow; he received nourishment through a tube inserted into his stomach.

When Alice Tutor saw him he was a pathetic ten-month old who weighed only nine pounds, so weak he could hardly move. She wondered if he would disturb her elderly patients. To which the doctor replied, "Weldon will never bother anyone. He is brain dead—a vegetable. We don't expect him to live."

Little did he know what would happen when the other patients took Weldon on as a project, loving him, caressing him, soothing him, giving him love and encouragement. Alice was sure "What this baby needs is love. He needs to know that someone cares if he lives or dies."

Little by little TLC worked its magic. This exciting story was written up by Patricia Skalka in the November 1984 issue of *Reader's Digest*. Eventually he was able to raise his tiny arms and make two fists. Then he was able to raise his head off the pillow, to gurgle, smile and cry. And then he took his first nourishment by mouth. Finally he was able to propel himself up and down the corridors in a baby walker. Can you imagine the excitement in that nursing home? The residents dropped nickels and dimes into a jar to buy toys for the boy and each one volunteered to baby-sit. Every day Weldon grew stronger. He became a smiling, affectionate child, eager for attention. Even the patients who had seemed withdrawn and responded to no one else, loved Weldon. He crawled from one chair to another for the residents to play with him. This is such a beautiful story of the healing power of love. Surely love does work miracles.

R: LOVE

"Love to be taken regularly in large doses" were the actual words on the prescription blank the doctor handed to Jimmy's mother.

Jimmy had been suffering from frequent stomach upsets. Doctors are discovering more and more that children's stomach disorders are caused by emotional upsets which often reflect a lack of love in the home. Little children are very susceptible to an atmosphere of irritability, impatience and anger which may make them feel unloved and even to blame for the problems of the parents.

Jimmy's stomach upsets started the spring he became a pitcher for his Little League team. He was a good pitcher but he began to be afraid to play for fear of losing. He felt his parents were proud of him only when he won. The stomach upsets arrived with every game.

The doctor, being unusually perceptive, was able to recognize the emotional basis of Jimmy's trouble. He was able to show the parents that their good little boy who was so eager to please was not a happy child. They, in turn, learned to be more patient with the boy's failures and show him that their love did not depend upon his winning. They followed the doctor's prescription and gave him "love, in large doses." Jimmy's stomach trouble was cured by love.

DOCTORS AGREE THAT LOVE CAN CURE THE SICK

Top doctors agree that love can work miracles. When the wonder drugs fail and modern medical science is stymied, the experts find that love can cure the sick.

A top neurosurgeon has stated, *Love is the most powerful force known to man. Never underestimate love's healing power, whether it be for a simple cold or a critical disease.*

A Harvard psychiatrist agrees: *I know of no illness, however slight or severe, including cancer, heart disease, diabetes and arthritis that cannot benefit from love.*

An outstanding surgeon has said, *Every disease can be cured by love. I think that 100 percent of all patients can improve with love. Love is more important than penicillin or other antibiotics. It is the greatest medication in the world.*

Dr. Smiley Blanton in his great book *Love or Perish* has this to say about the need for love:

As I look back over the long, full years, one truth emerges clearly in my mind—the universal need for love. Whether they think they do or not, all people want love. Their spoken words may tell of other things, but the psychiatrist must listen to their unconscious voice as well. He must probe deeply into the human mind and heart, for it is his function to evaluate the buried urges that determine our lives even though we often have no conscious knowledge of them whatsoever. There he sees that people sit on the threshold of their personalities, as Robert Louis Stevenson put it, and call on the world to come and love them. They cannot survive without love: they must have it or they will perish.

LOVE IS INNATE TO EVERY PERSON

Love is the greatest word in any language. Why? Because love is universal. Love is innate to every person. Many suppress it, bury it under fear, greed and anxiety, or kill it by hate. But yet it is there, ready to be kindled or rekindled when it is drawn upon to be expressed.

Love is a healer, a revealer of the truth. Love can open prison doors and open hearts, even a heart hardened by greed and fear such as a Scrooge. Hate destroys everything it touches, but love can build cities and undergird the welfare of a country.

Franklin P. Jones said, *Love doesn't only make the world go 'round. Love is what makes the ride worthwhile.* Yes, anything that is done in love brings joy and peace. Along the same line, Robert Browning remarked, *Take away love and our earth is a tomb.*

People sometimes say, "How can I love him after what he has done?" Many people felt this way and still feel this way about Hitler, Mussolini and other tyrants. Mahatma Gandhi led the people of India out of bondage to the British Empire by utilizing this approach, *Hate the sin and love the sinner.* You can love the person and still abhor what he is doing. Loving the person protects the center of love within from being destroyed by hate.

LOVE HEALS A MISUNDERSTANDING

A woman told me how she had hated a woman in her neighborhood because of a certain thing this woman did to her. She carried this burden in her heart for over two years and one day she decided to get rid of it by forgiving the woman. She telephoned her and took her out to lunch. They had a delightful time. At the conclusion of the lunch, her friend (newly restored) gave her a business lead which in turn earned her several thousand dollars. Many times the person for whom the grudge is held does not even know it. Such a waste of emotional activity on the negative side! Love healed the breach in this case.

Recently we were visiting a friend in a remote place in the desert. I asked about water, where did they get it? The answer was, "We had to drill for it and we found it because it was there." Isn't that the way it is with love? It's there in each one of us but sometimes we have to drill for it to get it up out of the depths where we have let it remain buried. In order to love, we must think love and feel love. This is how we draw it up from out of the depths.

WE DRAW FROM AN INFINITE SOURCE

Our confusion lies in thinking that the object of our love draws the love out of us. One does not fall in love but one draws upon the source of love within and directs it to the object of love. Since we are drawing from an infinite source we can have a universe of objects. In other words, we can love everyone but that does not mean that we have to like everything that they do.

Often we neglect making ourselves the object of our love. When we realize that we are created by God and that we are wonderful, mental and physical instruments for living, fed from an infinite source of divine love which is God, then we realize our mistake in overlooking loving ourselves. When we love ourselves, it becomes easier to love others. *Love the Lord thy God with all thy heart, and with all thy soul, and with all thy mind, and love thy neighbor as thyself.* is the great commandment.

In a talk before a half-million farmers in Czestochowa, Poland, which was reprinted in the November 1, 1982, issue of the *New Yorker* magazine, Ignacy Tokarczak, a Polish bishop, said: *Among those supreme values is love. Our nation believes in love. We shudder at the very mention of hatred or revenge, even against those who have brought us the greatest suffering and continue to do so. This is because our nation knows that love is a constructive force which conquers the world, along with faith.*

In this world in which there appears to be many troubled people and many troubled spots, it becomes necessary to bring love into play. People fight out of fear and they kill out of fear but remember, *perfect love casts out fear.* It is through love that we are born again into a consciousness of universal peace. So let's identify with love and make it a part of our whole being.

Your Statement of Love

I love the Lord my God right within me and within everyone. I am made whole and made one with all mankind through the perfect love that lives through me.

The will of God in me is health, but I must fill my heart with thoughts that produce health. The appearance of sickness is but the effect of sick thoughts. There is no power in symptoms, conditions, or any of the false appearances called dis-ease. As I turn to the Lord, my God, at the very center of my being, loving this law of perfect life, with all my heart, all my soul, and all my might, there is no room in me for thoughts that outpicture as dis-ease. The will of God in me is health, wholeness of mind, body and estate and this wholeness only will I serve until it outpictures in every facet of my life and I am made every whit whole. And so it is.

—*Your Needs Met*, p. 79.

7

LOVE IS IRRESISTIBLE

> *Love is patient and kind; love is not jealous or boastful;*
> *it is not arrogant or rude. Love does not insist on its own*
> *way; it is not irritable or resentful; it does not rejoice at*
> *wrong, but rejoices in the right. Love bears all things,*
> *believes all things, hopes all things, endures all things. Love*
> *never ends.*
> *So faith, hope, love abide, these three; but the greatest*
> *of these is love.*[1]

One time I put the power of love to a test in a jewelry store
during the busy after-Christmas rush season, when everyone
was exchanging gifts. I had come in to exchange a piece of
silverware, which the sales person had assured me I could
do, so I sought out the same sales person and explained my
problem to her.

I was tired and hurried and she was attempting to wait on
several customers at once. Before the transaction really got

[1]1 Cor. 13:4–8, 13 (RSV).

under way we were literally bristling at each other. She seemed to be consumed with fury toward me and I began to resent her.

Then I remembered something that I had heard not long before. All of a sudden, I felt at peace with myself as I remembered an inspiring talk in which the speaker had suggested that we make an experiment to find how easy it is to have people love us and cooperate with us.

Here it was within my power to free her and myself by trying this interesting experiment. I suppose I felt sorry for this disturbed little woman, and with this sympathy came a rush of love toward her. I reasoned thus: "We are one in God. Together we exist in divine mind sharing the same intelligence, using the same mind, completely surrounded by infinite love which leaves no room for resentment or discord. Since we are one, how can there be friction between us? There is no friction. There is only peace and harmony. The love of God flowing through us establishes us right now in harmony, peace and perfect right action."

So thoroughly was I convinced of this that I wasn't a bit surprised to see my ruffled friend coming back with my package with a smile on her face. She held out her hand and said, "I want to thank you for being so patient with me. I am sorry I was irritable and I hope you'll come back and see me sometime."

This was a victory for me. I'd drawn the larger circle and both of us were happy because of it. I walked out of that store fairly glowing with the joy and satisfaction that comes with this sort of success. People turned and smiled at me in the elevator and on the street. Later that afternoon I completed a very successful business transaction. It seemed no one could resist me for there was no resistance in me. I was feeling one with all mankind and all mankind was feeling one with me.

It's really so simple. Nothing complicated is required, only enough reasoning to make you yourself possess a strong feeling of love for the other person. Love is so impelling no one can resist it.

Ernest Holmes wrote, *If one makes himself receptive to the idea of love, he becomes lovable. To the degree that he embodies love, he is love; so people who love are loved.*[2]

HOW TO LOVE THOSE WHO SEEM HARD TO LOVE

"I understand the definition of love; I have read books and articles, and have heard sermons and discussions about love, yet, how can I love? People are so hard to love."

I am reading from a letter that I received in the mail.

Here is another. It opens: "My daughter-in-law is doing everything she can to ruin my son's life." There followed page upon page of the most venomous attack on a person that I have ever read. I almost expected the pages to burn up in my fingers. At the end of the letter, this mother-in-law writes, "I know you're going to tell me that I must love my daughter-in-law, but how can I love that woman?"

Edgar is an elderly man in a rest home. He is not there by choice. His rather frail daughter has finally come to the point where she can no longer work all day and take care of her father at night. The father is bitter. He hates everybody there, the supervisor, the nurses, his roommate, and above all his daughter who put him in that place.

[2]Ernest Holmes, *The Science of Mind*, (New York: Dodd, Mead, 1938).

Every day my mail convinces me over and over that there is only one answer to every human problem, only one panacea to every human ill: love. Hate and resentment separate us from each other and from life.

Down deep in their hearts, the people who write me know that love is the answer to their problems, but they just have no idea as to how to go about loving. The question is, how to love? How does a person make the break from hate or resentment over to love? Is it possible? Yes, it is. There are definite ways to accomplish this.

The first thing that one must realize is that it is not the object of the hate that is causing the hate, or a resentful person causing your resentment. It is the absence of love in your heart.

Each person is a center of love, whether he knows it or not. *God did not give us a spirit of timidity but a spirit of power and love and self-control.*[3] It is up to us to think of ways to express this love. It is up to us to draw the larger circle.

A friend of mine told me of a wonderful experience that changed her life. She said that as children she and her sister had hated each other. Let's call them Carol and Betty. Betty, three and a half years younger, was Daddy's little darling. Carol, who had been the apple of the father's eye, was now left out in the cold. Therefore, little Betty was her enemy. These two little girls shared a bed. They slept at opposite edges of the bed, and if Betty would accidentally touch Carol with her toe, Carol would shriek, "Don't touch me!"

Then one day the grownup Carol told me that something happened that caused her to feel loving toward Betty. She said that she would never forget the experience. They were sitting on the opposite sides of the back seat of the family

[3] 2 Tim. 1:7 (RSV).

automobile en route to a swimming party. All of a sudden, Carol said that she felt a wonderful feeling of love well up inside her. She became aware of the birds singing, the beautiful blue sky, the wildflowers along the way, and life became entirely different. Without realizing what she was doing, she reached over and put her arm around her sister's waist. Never again could she hate her sister. Today they are very close. Carol had drawn the larger circle and both of the sisters had been blessed by it.

THE ONE WHO GIVES REAPS THE GREATEST REWARD

A woman in a rest home told me that she hated every moment of it until one day one of the nurses came up to her and asked if she would read the newspaper to a blind man. "Well, I'll give it a try," she replied. Reluctantly she took the paper and approached him as he sat gloomily by the window in his wheelchair. "All of a sudden," she said, "it came to me that he could not even see the flowers in the garden." With a new feeling of warmth and compassion, she asked him which part of the paper he would like to hear.

At that moment there began an unusually fine friendship between two lonely people. She found that he was brilliant and was a good conversationalist, and they engaged in wonderful conversations and shared so much. Before they were through she was reading the paper from the first page to the last, and discussing just about every article in it with him. She exclaimed, "I gained far more than I gave." Before long she became known as the "rest home angel," because she found ways to share with just about everyone in the rest home. It became one of the happiest times in her life. Love is irresistible. Love can accomplish wonders when we are willing to draw the larger circle and take others in.

LOVE IS ALREADY THERE

Love has to begin right within us. Each one has to make a move, be it ever so slight, in the direction of love.

Sometimes it starts with understanding. But there has to be the desire to understand. I find that this can be accomplished by a simple affirmation: "I understand you and you understand me." When I find someone who seems hard to love, I work at this, and when I begin to understand that person, then I begin to love that person.

Love can start with compassion. The word *compassion* is derived from the root meaning *with love*. Instead of looking at a person derisively or condemningly, just because that person is different, try compassion. How would you feel in that person's shoes, and what would you need to help you feel loved? It is in giving that we receive, and we can feel love only as we give love.

LOVE CAN BE EXPRESSED IN LITTLE WAYS

So many people think that when they are trying to develop a feeling of love they have to do something tremendous, that there has to be a great change. It's through the little things, developing a feeling of gentleness or kindness toward each other, that we learn the ways of love. Jesus said, *Inasmuch as ye have done it unto one of the least of these my brethren, ye have done it unto me.*[4] When we express love in little ways; just the casual giving of a smile, going back to say a good word, the little things that we do in the spirit of love; these are the things that make up the total idea of love. This is the way we begin to love. Finally, we are able to live love in all areas of our expression.

We have to keep remembering that love begins right within our own hearts. We have to change *our* attitudes, *our* posture, and change our whole thought into a feeling of a desire to love. The more we love, the more love will come to us. The reason love was given to us as a commandment was for our own sakes, not for the sake of others. It is expedient to us that we love. Our whole life, our happiness, our health, our everything depends upon how we love.

ONE OF LOVE'S ENEMIES

Adela Rogers St. Johns once told me that she felt that the greatest enemy of love was indifference. The more I thought about it, the more I realized that she really had something there. Love lives in and through each one of us. It's like electric power lying dormant. We have to turn the switch. It's there, but it's not ours until we accept it and use it. As the poet said, we then can win by drawing the larger circle that takes others in.

[4]Mt. 25:40.

GOD IS LOVE

God is love and when we love we are in the heart of God. Compared to the love of God, our own feeble attempts at loving may seem a watered down version, but even a little moving in the direction of love is a shortcut to God.

To love is to partake of the very nature of God, to be one with God.

St. Augustine became aware of love the hard way, through struggle and long years of a feeling of separation, but once he understood the knowledge of the love of God, he told all who would listen: *"Love and do what you will."* The heart that is filled with love is incapable of sin, or hurting others. Having had the spiritual experience of oneness with love we are never again satisfied without it. *"My heart is restless 'til it rests in Thee,"* exclaimed St. Augustine.

LOVE SUSTAINS US

The knowledge of the love of God is an experience so overwhelming that once known, all else pales by comparison. Never again are we content without it. It becomes our primal goal, for out of it comes every other gift. Love is all-inclusive. Every small attempt on our part to let the love of God express through us brings us closer to the ultimate cosmic experience of all-inclusive love.

Love is the divine panacea for every human ill. Love never fails. Love never falters. Love embraces all. Love forgives all. Love swallows up all of our failures and gives us back its grace. It is so freely given. When we are willing to take the first step, love does it all for us. Love asks only that we turn in its direction, that we be willing for the wonder and the glory to take place in us.

We who thought of ourselves as lonely and forsaken have been loved since the beginning of time. *Yea, I have loved thee with an everlasting love, therefore with lovingkindness have I drawn thee...And their soul shall be as a watered garden and they shall not sorrow anymore at all.*[5]

Your Statement of Love

...but the greatest of these is love.[6]

Of all the attributes of God, love is the one least understood and most needed to be understood. Love is the answer to every human need. Love transcends all limitation and transforms our problems into victories.

Love is everywhere present in all of life. Love heals, protects and guides.

I draw love from an infinite source everytime I consciously give forth love. Every problem in my life is but an opportunity to give forth more love. If people seem to be difficult, I silently bless them until enemies become friends—friends who have caused me to experience more love. There is no problem which love cannot heal. For this I give thanks. And so it is.

—*Your Needs Met*, p. 93.

[5]Jer. 31:3,12.
[6]1 Cor. 13:13 (RSV).

8

LOVE IS FORGIVENESS

Let us then try what love will do—Force may subdue,
but love gains, and he who forgives first wins.
—William Penn

Every morn and every night, some are born to sweet delight.
Every morn and every night, some are born to endless night. Every
night and every morn, some to misery are born, wrote William
Blake in the eighteenth century. Some people do seem
destined to be miserable, but years of one-to-one counsel-
ing convinced me that the miserable ones are held in a bondage of their own making. Invariably their jailors are
bitterness, hate and resentment. I have seen many such
people transformed through forgiveness. Those who remain
in bondage do so because they prefer to hang onto their
bitterness.

HATE IS DESTRUCTIVE

"I feel that I am being destroyed by the cancer of hate," writes one of my correspondents who is honest enough to take a good look at herself and brave enough to want to do something about it. Most people are not yet ready to admit that their hates might be destroying them; that hidden resentment might be responsible for the problems they experience.

Love, Paul said, *is the fulfilling of the law.* Hate is the opposite of love. Hate separates us from our lifeline which is love. Just as a plant deprived of food and water will begin to disintegrate, so do we begin to show the effects of this separation in our bodies and our life experience. *We cannot afford the luxury of hate for a single instant.* If there is some problem in your life that persists, I advise you to start taking an inventory of your "little hates," for even the little resentments add up until they become dangerous.

"But, I have a right to hate that person!" you say. "Look what he did to me!" You may have the right from a human standpoint, but can you afford to hate him? Can you afford to separate yourself from God? Would you rather be justified or healed? Would you like to take a shortcut to being healed? There is one—love.

It has been said, and rightly so, that Jesus was the master psychologist. In the Sermon on the Mount Jesus discusses every kind of block that man is prone to set up for himself: resistance; conceit; undue value placed upon material things; anxiety for the future, etc. But to one mistake he gives special consideration. Since the Sermon on the Mount might well be called "Rules for Right Living," one might conclude that the instructions given by Jesus on the matter of forgiveness were to him the most important part of realigning one's self with the power of God.

FORGIVENESS IS THE KEY TO LOVE

The surest way to block our prayers is to hold a grudge. To have any feeling of getting even with another, any thought of resentment against anyone, is to block the unfoldment of Spirit in our lives. We all want to be effective in our prayer work; there is no part of life that is more essential to a person's well-being than to feel that his prayers are effective. It is therefore most important that we get rid of anything in our thinking which nullifies our prayers.

Let us see what the greatest psychologist of all had to say about this:

> So if you are offering your gift at the altar, and there remember that your brother has something against you, leave your gift there before the altar and go; first be reconciled to your brother, and then come and offer your gift.[1]

And in the next two verses Jesus advises us:

> Make friends quickly with your accuser, while you are going with him to court, lest your accuser hand you over to the judge, and the judge to the guard, and you be put in prison; truly, I say to you, you will never get out till you have paid the last penny.[2]

[1]Mt. 5:23,24 (RSV).
[2]Mt. 5:25,26 (RSV).

One gets the impression that Jesus considered holding a grudge to be pretty expensive business and that it was not worthwhile praying at all while one was holding resentment against one's brother. He tells us also that when we pray we are to enter into the closet of the mind, the secret place within, and when we have shut the door, we are to pray to the Father which sees in secret; and the Father which sees in secret shall reward us openly. That is to say, that it is highly important that our minds be free from any sense of separation, any sense of impingement from without; that only when we have shut the door behind us on our resentments, our hostilities, our grudges, are we ready to commune with the Father whose nature is love.

And right here we are given the beautiful Lord's Prayer which is used by all Christian churches, and in the center of the prayer is further instruction on forgiveness:

And forgive us our debts, as we also have forgiven our debtors.[3]

It is clear that Jesus considered it very important that we forgive before we could expect our own mistakes to be forgiven. Verse 14 of this chapter goes on with this discussion on forgiveness:

For if you forgive men their trespasses, your heavenly Father also will forgive you; but if you do not forgive men their trespasses, neither will your Father forgive your trespasses.[4]

[3]Mt. 6:12 (RSV).
[4]Mt. 6:14,15 (RSV).

WHAT FORGIVENESS REALLY MEANS

Forgiveness really means to give up any feeling, any resentment or hate against the self or against another, or against life. Does that surprise you? People actually do resent God when they resent what life has done to them. Even as they pray, people often think, "God, why did this have to happen to me?" So even in this prayer they are entertaining a feeling of resentment against God for letting this thing happen to them. Of course, we know that actually God has never done anything against them at all. God cannot do anything against us. God is love, everywhere present. How can love be against love?

Man, the image and likeness of God, the very expression of God, is one with the Presence; but only his recognition of his oneness will bring unity into his experience. There is, in truth, no way for man to be against God, or God against man. Man, however, sets up false premises that act against his highest good, such as when he resists some evil experience that he has in reality brought upon himself, falsely ascribing it to the "will of God," and then setting about to resent the difficulty as coming from God. When we understand that God is not a man up in the sky dishing out rewards and punishments, but the law of infinite goodness, we come to see that it is just man against himself. We see, then, that all of our troubles are the result of setting up division, a sense of separation right within our own thinking. It is only through forgiveness that we are able to become one with life again.

WHY SOME PRAYERS ARE NOT ANSWERED

Ye did run well; who did hinder you that ye should not obey the truth?[5]

Many times we wonder why our prayers seem ineffective. Some have called them "dry prayers," others have called them "hollow prayers." The question comes up every now and then: "What is wrong with my prayers? Why aren't my prayers answered?" Then, we need to ask ourselves, *What did hinder you that ye did not obey the truth?* Have we possibly brought our gift to the altar without making peace within ourselves first? If so, the gift is tainted by that subtle thought of separation.

The reason that forgiveness is so important is that if we hold a grudge against another, we hold it against ourselves. As Dr. Ernest Holmes so aptly put it, *From selfish reasons alone, if from no loftier reason, we cannot afford to find fault, to hate, or even to hold in mind anything against any living soul! The God of love cannot hear the prayer of the one who fails to love.*[6]

THE ETERNAL QUESTION

Many people ask, "How can I love?" As we have said before, the answer is *start with understanding.* Know that the one who seems the hardest to love would not be that way if he could help it. He needs your love the most.

[5]Gal. 5:7.
[6]Ernest Holmes, *The Science of Mind,* (New York: Dodd, Mead, 1938).

Love is a fire that kindles its first embers in the narrow nook of the private bosom, tossing a wandering spark out of another private heart, glows and enlarges until it forms and feeds upon the multitudes of men and women, upon the universal heart of all, and so lights the whole world and all nature with its generous light.

—Ralph Waldo Emerson

It is that little gift of understanding that comes into our hearts when we feel in harmony with life. We feel that God is present in every part of life. We are one with all of life as we feel our communion with our fellow man. No man is an island. We take our love from the infinite source that binds us together as one.

A PRACTICAL EXAMPLE

In his book *The Miracle of Mind Power*, Dan Custer tells this story:

When someone hurts us and we carry the memory of that hurt throughout the year, we come to have the feeling of being rejected by all of life. Mr. Allison, a man of sixty, told me he never had been a success because twenty-eight years earlier his business partner had absconded with the money of their partnership. He blamed his failure in life on the defection of this old partner. I suggested that he forgive the old partner and thereby remove every excuse for failure.

Some two or three years later this same man attended a class I was giving in human relations. One evening he asked to speak to the class. He told his story: for twenty-eight years he had blamed his failure in life on a partner who had absconded with his money. He explained that I had told him to forgive that old experience and to pray for the good of this partner whom he had not seen for many years. "I didn't know how to pray for him but I decided to wish him all the good that I wanted for myself so I did it in my own simple way. I have always wanted a good automobile and I like to smoke good cigars. So, in my imagination I saw this old partner driving up the street in a fine Cadillac, smoking a big cigar. In my imagination I called to him. He stopped. He seemed a bit embarrassed; but I said, 'Bill, it is all right. I understand. I forgive you. I hold nothing against you. I am glad you are successful. I am glad that you have the very things I like myself. The old experience is forgiven and forgotten. You are free and I am glad you are, for I have freed myself'."

Mr. Allison went on to say that immediately his affairs took a turn for the better and now he was financially quite successful and very happy.[7]

Dr. Custer says that the way to release the other person is to take the incident into your consciousness and analyze it until you finally come to understand. He suggests that every time the other person's name comes into your mind, you bless him and release him until you eventually have a different feeling about him.

FORGIVENESS OILS THE LOCK

Resentment of any kind tends to block the flow of creative life in our experience. It sometimes seems that a door has been locked against us. The key is love. Forgiveness oils the

[7]Dan Custer, *The Miracle of Mind Power*, (Englewood Cliffs, N.J.: Prentice-Hall, 1960).

lock and love opens the door to the kingdom of all good. It makes no difference what the object of our resentment is. Some resent themselves, some even resent God. It is not the object that is to blame; it is only our feeling of misunderstanding that is making the sense of separation. The answer is to give up the feeling of resentment and let understanding take its place.

As we enter into scientific prayer, turning away from the appearances, turning to divine love, it is necessary that we do so with a free mind, a mind not burdened with resentment, anxiety or fear, a mind that is free from the chains of frustration.

A New York doctor reports that of all the people who came to him, 70 percent were suffering from resentment.

> Lo, this only have I found, that God hath made man upright; but they have sought out many inventions.[8]

One of these inventions that seems to keep us from reaching emotional maturity is resentment. Having invented it, we must learn how to get rid of it. Anything that stands between us and our highest good is a false god. When a person holds a grudge he actually is worshipping his resentment. The results are always tragic.

A TRUE STORY

A man in one of my classes finally realized this. He told me that he had actually been worshipping hate. The word *worship* means *to assign great worth to*, and this man saw that

[8]Eccl. 7:29.

he had been assigning great worth to hate and that it was destroying him. He said that he had let an old grudge interfere with his career. It seems that when he was in high school he had been a star on the football team, until one of the players on the team set out to undermine him so that he did not get to play in a certain big game. He felt that the other boy had cut him out in order to get the glory and honor for himself. He was determined to get even. It became an obsession with him.

All through college, instead of promoting his own activities, he spent his time trying to get even with the other chap until it became his full time occupation. At last, they graduated from college and, lo and behold, they went into the same profession. Resentment was still the ruling motive in his life; always this other fellow was the object of his desire to get even. He would go along for a while on an even keel and then something would remind him of his unhappy experience back in high school and a sort of ugliness would come over him. He said he didn't do well in his work and he wasn't happy in his home life.

And then one day he realized that this thing had become a sort of mental cancer that was destroying him. This was when he came to me. We talked it out and prayed it out together. He could see that he had been obstructing the creative flow of life by his desire to get even. He was able to go to his friend and talk to him. Imagine his surprise to find that the other fellow was entirely ignorant of the whole thing. He could not even recall what events had transpired. It all seemed rather ridiculous. They became close friends. And now our friend was able to move ahead in his career. He did well from then on because he was completely at peace with himself.

There are so many cases where people have carried grudges for years solely on the premise that they had to get even. But there is no getting even. Only the hater is hurt. As someone has said, *Hate is a bonfire that scorches the ground it burns on.*

REVISE THE PAST

We have seen that it is impossible to wipe out the past. Our mental tape recorder preserves it. Yes, but we *can* revise the past. We can pour so much love and understanding on the memory of a past incident that it is completely neutralized. It can actually become a good memory instead of a bad memory. We don't have to let old animosities stand between us and our fulfillment. When we have learned this lesson we have come a long way toward spiritual maturity.

How is it done? By understanding. No matter how hateful the other person may have been, we must start with understanding. Know that each person does what he does because he believes that it is the right thing to do at the moment. It may not be what you think is right, it may not be what society thinks is right; but at that moment it seems the best thing that he can do. Take a person who goes out and gets drunk. He causes a lot of misery for himself and maybe a lot of misery for his family, but at that moment, he thinks it is the only way that he can escape from himself.

Suppose a person robs a bank. He thinks it is the only way that he can get the money that he thinks he needs and so he, too, is doing what he thinks is best for him at the moment. It doesn't matter how well justified we are in condemning his action, it isn't going to do us any good to resent it. Actually, as we have seen, it is going to do us a great deal of harm. The first step, then, is to realize that we don't want to take on this kind of thinking. Say to yourself, "That's *his* problem. I'm not going to make it *my* problem." As Emmet Fox explained in one of his books—if you saw a little child who was unable to reach a high shelf, you wouldn't condemn him for it, you'd know that in time he would grow. So it is with spiritual infants—we have to give them time to grow. What a privilege it is to know that we can help them silently and, in helping them, free ourselves. To quote Emmet Fox:

> Setting others free means setting yourself free, because resentment is really a form of attachment. It is a Cosmic Truth that it takes two to make a prisoner; the prisoner and the gaoler. When you hold resentment against anyone, you are bound to that person by a cosmic link, a real, though mental chain. You are tied by a cosmic tie to the thing that you hate...You must cut all such ties, by a clear and spiritual act of forgiveness. You must loose him and let him go. By forgiveness you set yourself free; you save your soul. And because the law of love works alike for one and all, you help to save his soul too, making it just so much easier for him to become what he ought to be.[9]

I find it helps to understand that evil is neither person, place nor thing, it is just nothing trying to be something, inverted thinking that has temporarily gotten the upper hand. Error may seem to be using a person, but error is not that person.

[9]Emmet Fox, *The Sermon on the Mount* (New York: Harper & Row, 1938).

Is there someone in your life whom you find it hard to forgive? Try blessing him. Bless the spirit of truth within him. Pray for him. Say to yourself: *The Christ in me salutes the Christ in you. The Christ in me understands the Christ in you. I forgive you. I bless you. I free you. I understand you and you understand me. I release you to your highest good.*

HEALING THROUGH FORGIVENESS IS A PROVEN FACT

The past must be forgiven before a person can accept a healing. We are coming more and more to see that forgiveness is an "open sesame" to answered prayer.

The late Dr. Masaharu Taniguchi, founder of the Seicho-No-Ie Foundation in Japan, had millions of followers. He taught them, *Reconcile yourself with everyone, with everything in the universe. Give thanks for all things. Not just in some easygoing situations, but in all situations.*

In his book *You Can Heal Yourself,*[10] he tells of case after case where forgiveness was the answer. Sometimes a person needed to forgive a husband or wife, sometimes he had resented himself. In almost every case of the miraculous healings he reported there was some emotional block that needed to be dissolved. The healing followed easily and naturally. In every case there was some reconciliation needed. Love was the healer.

[10] Masaharu Taniguchi, *You Can Heal Yourself*, (Tokyo: Seicho-No-Ie Foundation, 1961).

BUT HAVE WE FORGIVEN GOD?

Sometimes long after we have forgiven others, and even forgiven ourselves, we continue to feel that there has been some form of injustice in our experience. We feel that some situation just wasn't fair. Over and over again we hear people say, "Why did this have to happen to me?"

Life evolves, with mathematical precision, projecting into manifestation the thoughts that we involve. God did not take your child away from you. In some way we cannot understand, the law of life was working for that little soul, taking it on to its next experience, its next classroom for spiritual instruction.

God did not cause your business to fail. This experience can be turned into great good if you will seek the lesson that it brings you. Truly, *all things work together for good to them that love God, to them who are the called according to his purpose.*[11] What is his purpose?—love shared, love made manifest, love everywhere present. Stop feeling that some injustice has been done to you. Start loving the Lord thy God right within you with all thy mind, with all thy strength, with all thy heart. Leave off being the prodigal son eating the husks with the swine. The moment you forgive the Father, you start back to the Father's house and the Father comes out to meet you. Then you are ready to sit down at the Father's table and eat of the feast.

[11]Rom. 8:28.

A WONDERFUL NEW LIFE AWAITS YOU

Now you are ready to become your true self, unimpeded by resentment, grudges, self-punishment, or any other mental block. Now you are free, ready to live a life that is whole and complete.

Your Statement of Love

Let us know together that there is only one power and that power is God right where you are. There is no power but of God. Love is all there is. Let us forgive ourselves of any past mistake, giving up all condemnation, letting go all sense of guilt. Let us realize right now that we are as innocent as babes because God is living through us. Let us love the spirit of truth in every one, loving our fellow man as we love ourselves, accepting him as the very extension of our lives for we are both the extension of God life. Let us love them that hate us, bless them that curse us, that we may be sons of God, aware that God is everywhere present. This is spiritual maturity! And so it is.

—Your Needs Met, p. 65.

9

GOD'S LOVE IS UNCONDITIONAL

*What is love?...It is the sweetness of life; it is the sweet,
tender, melting nature of God, flowing up through his seed
of life into the creature, and of all things making the
creature most like unto himself, both in nature and
operation.*

—*Isaac Pennington,* Works, *1681*

The wonderful thing about God's love is that it is completely unconditional. As the rain falls on the just and the
unjust, so the grace of God is poured out for all who will
receive it. It is man, himself, who conditions God's love by
hiding himself in a cave of doubt or fear; by doubting the
presence of God; by being anxious about tomorrow; by being anxious about his children and his fellow man; by hating
and resenting others; by being envious; and by loving things
and circumstances more than he loves God. In truth,
nothing can separate us from the love of God. Nothing can
interrupt the flow of divine goodness in life, but we must

turn, trustingly, to the source of all love in order to experience God's unconditional love.

GOD'S LOVE FOR *YOU* IS UNCONDITIONAL

God's love for you is unconditional. It makes no difference who you are, what your educational background has been, or who your ancestors were. You may be sinner or saint. It makes no difference where you are. Even if you have made your bed in hell, *Behold, thou art there!*[1] It makes no difference what you have done. You may be a person who has sinned against yourself and against society, in the sense that you have done things that have harmed yourself and others. Still, it makes no difference what you have done. God's love for you is unconditional.

God's love is perfect in and through His creation. We, being the image and likeness of God, can feel this love and know that it is there for us. We can start by recognizing the expression of love in the beauty of nature surrounding us. We begin to realize that this is God expressing His love. We can feel this love expressing through us. We are the image and likeness of God, that we, too, may love. *God is love, and when we love we are like Him.*

WE MUST LOVE AS GOD LOVES

If we would know this all-encompassing love, we must love as God loves. We must, as Kahlil Gibran says, *Give as in yonder valley the myrtle breathes its fragrance into space.* Gibran

[1]Ps. 139:8.

goes on to say, *Through the hands of such as these God speaks, and from behind their eyes He smiles upon the earth.*[2] How can we accept for ourselves the unconditional love if we are always conditioning it? We must love as God loves. We must let the love that lives through us flow freely, taking no note of the worthiness of the object, nor noting whether our love is being received. We must set no conditions upon our love, letting it go freely, knowing that it is from an infinite source. The mind and heart of man is the channel for infinite love, and the very power of God is released through this love.

ALL CREATION IS LOVE MANIFEST

God's love is always creative. It knows exactly what to do and how to do it. It is through love that all progress and advancements are made. Without love, no progress is made. That which is done without love soon fails and is eventually lost even to the memory of man.

The creativeness expressing in and through us is God's love, expressing in terms of creation. The tenderness that is expressed in and through us is God's love expressing itself in terms of tenderness. The joy expressing in and through us is God's love expressing as joy. The power that expresses in and through us is God's love expressing as power. The intelligence expressing in and through us is God's love expressing as intelligence. *Love is a many-splendored thing.* It expresses in a myriad of ways. Because it is infinite, its ways cannot be counted. Every part of creation is an expression of love in manifestation; yet each part is different. The Spirit

[2]Kahlil Gibran, *The Prophet* (New York: Alfred A. Knopf, 1936).

of God moves in and through life as the movement of love in and through its creation.

Every good gift and every perfect gift is from above, and cometh down from the Father of lights, with whom is no variableness, neither shadow of turning.[3] Every good gift comes into visible manifestation from the one great gift to us, the love of God. It comes to us as our needs met in wondrous ways. It becomes all that we need. As we give it forth in thought, action, or deed, this love is continually moving forward into expression, taking form in the way that is right for it.

If we think that God has abandoned us, we fail to recognize that at this very moment our need is being met. Perhaps this need is not being met in just the way that we have outlined that we want it to be met. This is because our interpretation of our needs is usually conditioned for the purpose of meeting some fear. We fear some happening; therefore we say that we have to have something to offset it. Because we do not trust God's perfect plan for us, we say, "I need to have this fulfillment now." It is then that we block the flow of infinite love living through us. When we demand that our need be met in some certain way, we condition the love that is unconditioned. We do not trust love when we say that it must come to us in some certain way.

God is able to make all grace abound toward you; that ye, always having all sufficiency in all things, may abound to every good work.[4] We let this illimitable love of God in and through us flow through us into expression when we are able to back away a bit from our need of the moment and say, "I surrender to thee, O Presence, I surrender to Thee, O Infinite

[3]Jas. 1:17.
[4]2 Cor. 9:8.

Father who knows all things. You know my needs. You knew my needs before I was ever aware of them. You knew them as already met. Answer my need in the way that is right, and I will be the expression of this need fulfilled."

Having gotten what Emerson calls our *bloated nothingness* out of the way, we are now in a position to let the unconditioned love of God flow further into our experience.

IN TRUTH THERE IS NOTHING TO HEAL

To God there is nothing to heal. God is *of purer eyes than to behold evil, and cannot look on iniquity*.[5] God's creation is perfect. It cannot lack in any way. God's love is unconditioned. God's love is perfect. Nothing in God's perfect life has ever been sick, encumbered, obstructed, or lacking in any way whatsoever. In truth, you have never been sick or sinful. You have never suffered or been contaminated in any way. Sin and sickness are dreams and delusions. Healing comes when we put ourselves in line with unconditioned love and accept for ourselves that which has been true for us all the time. The healing is there because we have never been separated from love. It just awaits our acceptance to become manifest in our experience. It is only our own feelings and thoughts that get in the way of our divine perfection becoming expressed. Fear, and the children of fear — anxiety, worry, jealousy, etc. — seem for a time to get in the way; but they are not the truth about us.

As we open the door and let love flow through us, live through us, express through us, fear is neutralized and cast out. God is already whole and perfect. Wholeness and

[5]Hb. 1:13.

90

perfection are re-established for us when we know that there is no power in the condition; that there is no power in the circumstance; that God's love does not recognize any power in condition or circumstance. God's love is free, and freely flows through life in its perfect way. That which we think of as a healing is the recognition that God is the only power, the only substance, the only being. That which has seemed to be less than perfect is not the truth.

WE ALONE SET UP THE QUALIFYING CIRCUMSTANCES

God loves us freely. God does not say to us that it is incumbent upon us that we read some certain books, join some certain religion, that we go to some certain place or do some certain things before he will let his love live through us. God's love is completely unconditioned. Therefore these conditions are not set up by God. They are our own temptations, things that we do to try to prove to ourselves that we are wise or that we know better than God. It is only as we are able to get our human limitations out of the way that we are able to accept the glorious gift of unconditioned love. This was the awareness that John had when he said, *Greater is he that is in you, than he that is in the world.*[6] This is what Jesus meant when he said, *Of myself I do nothing, the Father that dwelleth in me, he doeth the works.*[7] This was the understanding that Paul had when he said, *Christ in you, the hope of glory.*[8] Say to yourself:

[6] 1 Jn. 4:4.
[7] John 14:10.
[8] Col. 1:27.

"Christ, the love of God, living in and through me, knows me better than I know myself. And so, I let the Christ, God's perfect love individualized in me, express through me. I trust God's unconditioned love to bless me, provide for me, and perfect that which is given me to do."

THE PART WE PLAY

Here is where our will comes in. As Glenn Clark once said, we must declare, *I will to will the will of God.* Our will is our discipline of ourselves, our refusing to accept ourselves as weak, tempted, the recipient of fear, or the breeder of fear. We must take command of the situation and, using our God-given intelligence and courage, say, "Get thee behind me Satan. You are the lie and the father of them. Get out of my life. You are not of me. I will have no part of you." Satan is the untruth, the false belief, or error.

It is in this way that we strike out the thing that seems to have been impeding us, that seems to have been holding us back. How can we do it? By recognizing that God's love cannot be dammed up by any condition. God's wholeness and perfection cannot be dammed up by circumstance, condition or personality. It is we who have tried to hold back our own good, like King Canute who stood by the shore and tried to hold back the tide. The result is that we destroy ourselves when all the time we could be living by Grace, letting God's unconditioned love flow through us into perfect expression. As the voice of Jesus said to Paul on the road to Damascus, *Saul, Saul, why persecutest thou me? It is hard for thee to kick against the pricks.*[9] Let us leave off our

[9]Acts 9:4,5.

foolish resistance, our feeble attempts to carry the responsibility of God and instead flow with the tide of unconditioned love by saying:

> "I surrender to Thee, O infinite Presence, that knows all things and is willing to live through me. I remove my self-imposed limitations. I am willing to receive Thy unconditioned good."

HOW, THEN, DO WE ESCAPE FROM BONDAGE?

We walk out of our self-imposed bondage by turning our attention to God. We find that we were our own jailers. We turn our attention away from the condition or problem and turn completely to God, the infinite, the perfect. We keep knowing over and over that God's love is unconditional. It never at any time questions us as to why we do something or what we are planning in the future. It only says, "Here I am. Accept me. Let me live through you." As we accept it, the conditions fall away. There is no power in them. We pull the rug right out from under them and they fall and break in a million pieces just like the big idol in the story of Daniel. It fell and crashed into a million pieces. Why? Because it was false. It had no power of its own. Walk out of your bondage. Accept your freedom. Deny the lie. Affirm the truth. Refuse to believe in limitation. Let love live through you in its perfect way and know the glory of a bright new day.

Your Statement of Love

God's love for me is not conditioned by who I am; by my occupation; by where I was born; by where I was educated; by what I have done in the past; or by what I have been planning to do in the future. God's love for me is not conditioned. It is not influenced by any circumstance, no matter what it may be. God's love for me is perfect and complete right now.

I don't have to make anything happen or change anything. It makes no difference where I am. God's love for me is so complete that He has given me of Himself; I am made in His image and likeness. The very power of God is the power of my life. The very Spirit of God is the spirit of my life. The very love of God is expressed in my life.

Wherever I am, God is. If I were in the middle of a huge city, where I did not know a soul, God's love would be there, ready to provide loving friends and all that I might need. It is not conditioned by where I am. In the middle of a desert, all alone, God's Love would be there. *Whither shall I go from thy spirit, whither shall I flee from thy presence?* Wherever I might be, God's love is there before me to prepare my way. And so it is.

10

PUTTING LOVE TO WORK

(Love Techniques)[1]

> *To bless a thing is to fill it with life. Life is expansion and the thing will expand and progress. To bless it is to enfold it warmly in your thought and feeling and consciously desire its fullest and most beautiful expression. To bless is to send forth a power which is of God and therefore omnipotent. To bless is to take an inward stance in relation to something. It is to speak the word of good and then to stand silently while the currents of life flow through the patterns of your thought. To bless is to release the hidden life in everything.*
>
> —Ervin Seale

Love is universal—it flows freely from life itself. Therefore each person becomes a reservoir of love. Each person has

[1]Technique: The systematic procedure by which a complex or scientific task is accomplished.—*The American Heritage Dictionary of the English Language.*

love in common with all other people. Love is the common denominator. It is impossible to be truly happy without love. Love becomes the basic necessity for a life of fulfillment.

PUTTING LOVE TO WORK

Now we can believe all these wonderful things about love in theory, and yet never experience love unless we let it express in our lives. And so we have developed what we call Twelve Love Techniques. The first one is:

I. PRACTICE RECEIVING LOVE FROM
THE INFINITE SOURCE.

You will find as you go along that the best way to receive love is to give love, that it is truly in giving that we receive love. However, it is impossible to give from an empty heart, and so it is well to meditate on God's love. The Bible speaks of it as the Grace of God. And whenever you see this word *Grace*, know that it means illimitable love, which means love that can never be exhausted. A good exercise in learning to understand love is to change the word *God* wherever you find it to the word *love*. You will find that your understanding of the nature of God is tremendously expanded by doing this.

Listen to the words of the monk Father Zossima in the book *The Brothers Karamazov.*[2] This was his dying admonition:

[2]Fyodor Dostoyevski, *The Brothers Karamazov*, 1879.

Love will teach us all things: but we must learn how to win love: it is a possession dearly bought with labour and time; for one must love not sometimes only, for a passing moment, but always. There is no man who doth not sometimes love: even the wicked can do that. And let not men's sin dishearten thee: love a man even in his sin, for that love is a likeness of the divine love, and is the summit of love on earth.

Now you are ready to share love—for only when you have meditated upon love and have some concept of the omnipresence of love are you ready to share it with others. There is a very simple technique for doing this. Try it on someone whom you consider hard to love.

II. Speak Love in Your Mind Until You Feel It for Yourself and for Others.

Now we realize that this is not always easy, especially when it comes to those whom you have judged impossible to love. It is something you are going to have to do consciously for a while. The key is "I love." Think in your mind: "I love you." It is not necessary to say it aloud, but think it in your mind. This activates or draws forth love from the reservoir of love within you. In order to love we must think love, feel love, express love and *be* love. It is not a matter of "I ought to love"; not "I will love"; not "I hope to love some day"; but "I love you now." You may not like what a person does; you may not approve of him, but you cannot afford to not love him. Think to yourself: "I love God in this person."

Dr. Harry A. Overstreet in his book *The Mature Mind*[3] writes:

> The love of a person implies not the possession of that person but the affirmation of that person. It means granting him, gladly, the full right to his unique humanhood. One does not truly love a person and yet seek to enslave him — by law or by bonds of dependence and possessiveness.

So we must ask ourselves: How are we using love? Does our love free our loved ones, strengthen and enrich them? Do we use love as a bribe or a weapon to manipulate others and gain our own ends? Are we too permissive in our love? Are we too willing to be a whipping boy for others, thus impoverishing them? Do we think that love means continually making sacrifices, "wearing our fingers to the bone" for those we love? Do we try to possess our loved ones, thus weakening and demoralizing them? Does our love insist that others be made in *our* image and likeness? Are we confusing love with appeasement? As we consider the ways of love we begin to see that it is not as simple as it seems.

Love must be freely given without any strings attached. But true love is not namby-pamby. It does not mean that we must always let the other person have his way. Love must not be used as an excuse because we fear to take a stand. Love does not necessarily mean giving another person all that he selfishly demands of us. Love does not mean permissiveness. Love is letting the Grace of God express through us without judgment, freely blessing all those with whom we come in contact.

[3]Harry A. Overstreet, *The Mature Mind*. (New York: W.W. Norton & Co., Inc., 1949).

Whether we realize it or not, we make a choice between some degree of love and some degree of hate every moment of the day. Each thought we think, each act we perform, from motives of love, sends forth vibrations of health, peace, strength and contentment into the stream of life. On the contrary, each hateful thought we think, or hateful act, has a tendency to tear down and destroy. *Blessed are the pure in heart* (those who have a consciousness of God's love) *for they shall see God.*[4] The "I love" technique produces that "pure in heart" consciousness so necessary for the spiritual union.

In order to love, we must think love and feel love. In this way we are using the power of love. We cannot all be Pitirim Sorokins or Gandhis, but we need not sit on the sidelines and gaze wistfully at those who have accomplished great things. There is something we can do now. We can start right where we are using the greatest power in the world. As you go along, you will understand more and more how to do this.

III. BLESS YOUR MIND AND BODY DAILY.

Long after we have learned to love others we often continue to blame and condemn ourselves. Most people are guilty of condemning that wonderful instrument, the temple of the living God, the body. Start today with a total blessing program. Bless your body. Use this Statement of Love daily:

I bless my body. It is the temple of God—pure spiritual substance. Every cell of my body is activated by divine in-

[4]Mt. 5:8.

99

telligence. Every organ in my body is regulated by the involuntary life within me, in perfect harmonious action. Each organ in my body is a perfect part of a perfect whole—the perfect wholeness that is God expressing as me. I bless my body and give thanks for it. It is a faithful servant provided and maintained to house the individualization of God known as myself. I bless my body and release it in perfect confidence to the Father within who neither slumbers nor sleeps in His care for me.[5] And so it is.

Right here we'd like to add that the woman for whom this statement was written used it faithfully and received a healing from not one, but three, so-called "incurable diseases." That is, the doctors had considered them incurable; heart condition, diabetes, leukemia, were the names they had been given. A year later she was the picture of health, an active, happy, well-adjusted person. By blessing her body she overcame a sense of condemnation which had literally made her ill.

IV. Love the Power of Love Within You—
 This Is Loving God Within.

The late Dr. Fritz Kunkel wrote in his book *In Search of Maturity:*[6]

A person who is God-centered is poised, secure, at ease. A person who is ego-centered tends to panic, is emotionally unstable and insecure, ill at ease and uncertain about himself. When we think of loving the Power of God within

[5]Jack and Cornelia Addington, *Your Needs Met*, p. 111.
[6]Fritz Kunkel, *In Search of Maturity*.

ourselves, we are setting up a program of becoming God-centered, or Love-centered. When we become God-centered, we become emotionally mature. Only then are we capable of love, of loving our neighbor and ourselves, forgiving another in our hearts, irrespective of who he is and what he has done, receiving from another without draining or depleting him, giving to another without overwhelming or obligating him. Only then are we able to release the past and become governed by the Love Principle now. Only then can we trust the self, the integrity and wisdom of the self so that we can be true to the self and others. Out of this God-centered Consciousness comes respect for the self, respect for others, the ability to be happy alone, a sense of mature responsibility, accepting the self for what we really are. We are able now to cast aside self-aggrandizement for there is no longer any need for it.

Dr. Kunkel has said it all. It is hard to add anything to his statement. This technique means putting love first in our lives in relation to ourselves and others. We must continually ask ourselves, "Is this the loving thing to do or say?"

V. Learn to Constantly Observe and Praise Life Divine Within All of Nature.

Recognizing God in His creation about us is a wonderful way to develop a consciousness of love.

Love all of God's creation, the whole and every grain of sand in it. Love every leaf, every ray of God's light. Love the animals, love the plants, love everything. If you love everything, you will perceive the Divine mystery in all things. Once you perceive it, you will begin to comprehend it better every day. And you will come at last to love the whole world with an all-embracing love.

—Fyodor Dostoyevski
The Brothers Karamazov

As we recognize God in His wonderful creation around us, we are recognizing the omnipresence, the essence of all life, for if God, love, is everywhere present, the only source and creator, God had to use the essence of life, love, to build His creation.

Take the little bee that organizes a city, that builds ten thousand cells for honey, twelve thousand cells for larvae, a holy of holies for the mother queen; a little bee that observes the heat and, when the wax may melt and the honey be lost, organizes the swarm into squads; puts sentinels at the entrances, glues the feet down, and then, with flying wings, creates a system of ventilation to cool the honey that makes an electric fan seem tawdry—a little honey bee that will cover twenty square miles in a field of flowers to gather its nectar.

And if a tiny bee can perform such wonders, who then are we, that we should question the guidance of God? Who guides the swallows as they return year after year to San Juan Capistrano, or the salmon that returns to its source to spawn? Lift up your eyes and you will behold the hand that supports the stars, the God who guides the planets without collision. The miracle is all around us, and as we take time to praise it, and marvel at it, we will feel the love of God, everywhere present.

In the next chapter we will continue with Technique VI, the Blessing Technique, which has helped hundreds of people to bring peace and understanding into their homes and offices. Long ago we gave up counting how many marriages were recreated through the use of this technique. It is a powerful technique; one which we should all understand and use at the slightest indication of inharmony in personal relationships.

YOUR STATEMENT OF LOVE

Love is the answer to world peace. Through love, I let peace begin with me. I send my love forth to all the world. My thought of love is reflected from one to another until I cannot even conceive of the blessing that started with me.

There is no stranger in the strange land. Love makes all men brothers. Since love is omnipresent, there is no black-hearted criminal, there is no hate-filled despot. Love is all in all, reconciling the world to peace. Love sees good in all and calls forth good in all.

I love God. I love my own individual expression of God. I love my neighbor in every part of the world. I understand him. I bless him. I praise him. I am one with him and he is one with me. Through love I am unified with all mankind. Love is like a cleansing fire that spreads throughout the world. Let there be love on earth and let it begin with me. And so it is.

—*Your Needs Met*, p. 153.

11

GETTING ALONG WITH DIFFICULT PEOPLE

(Love Techniques, cont'd)

Love is giving with no thought of getting. It is tenderness enfolding with strength to protect. It is forgiveness without further thought of the thing forgiven. It is understanding of the thing forgiven. It is understanding of human weakness, with knowledge of the true man shining through. It is quiet in the midst of turmoil. It is trust in God with no thought of self. The light in the mother's eyes, the glory in the sacrifice, the quiet assurance of protection.

It is in the expectation of our Father's promise coming true. It is the refusal to see anything but good in our fellow man. It is the glory that comes with selflessness and the power that comes with assurance of the Father's love for His children. It is the voice that says "no" to our brother, though "yes" might be more easily said. It is resistance to the world's lust and greed, thus becoming a positive law of annihilation to error.

Love...the one thing no one can take from us...the one thing we can give constantly and become increasingly rich in the giving. Love can take no offense, for it cannot know that which it does not of itself conceive. It cannot hurt or be hurt, for it is the purest reflection of God, good. It is the one eternal, indestructible force for good. It is the will of God, preparing, planning, proposing, always what is best for all His universe.

—Anon.

In our last chapter we discussed the first five Love Techniques of what we call a "Love Workshop"; that is, ways to put love to work and realize definite results in our everyday living. In this chapter we will take up techniques VI and VII.

VI. Using the Blessing Technique for Those Who Seem Hard to Love.

I remember so well the first time we ever assigned the Blessing Technique. We had been reading a little book by Frances Wilshire which suggested blessing those who seem hard to love. the author said, *Think of the person who seems hard to love and say: "I bless you and bless you and bless you. I praise you and praise you and praise you."*

We first assigned the Blessing Technique to a couple who were about to get a divorce. The sister of the young husband had called me. She was a member of my church, but her brother and his wife were not. She had begged me to see them as a last chance of bringing the couple together. She said that the wife had already purchased her plane ticket to go back home to her family in Tennessee. As I recall, she was going to take the plane the next day. She did not want to see a minister. She just wanted to leave. She was through, she figured, so why waste any more time. The husband was equally adamant. He, too, had "had it" regarding the marriage. But to please the sister who had begged them to see me they did agree to come.

They arrived at five o'clock in the afternoon. Everyone else had left the office and my wife and I were waiting for them. We felt their hostility the moment they came in. I could see at once that I had to see them separately. There was no point in being a third party to another family argument. So, I decided to see the husband first. This left the wife sitting out in the lounge with my wife. When I had heard his story the inspiration came to me to suggest that he try the Blessing Technique. I told him that this must be kept a secret. He was not to tell her, but that if he would try the Blessing Technique for a week he would see remarkable results. His face brightened and I realized that he really did not want the marriage to break up. Pulling out a sheet of plain white manuscript paper from my desk, I asked him, "What are the things you like about your wife?"

He pondered for some time as if, at that point, he could not find very much to like about her. Finally he said, "Well, she's honest." "Good," I said. "Let's start with that—honesty. Write it down. Number two?" After a few moments' thought he said, "She's clean and neat." He put down clean and neat. After that it got a little easier. He did allow that she was a pretty good cook and a good housekeeper. Before he was through he had been able to fill the first side of the sheet with things he could admire about his wife.

"Now," I told him, "we are going to turn the sheet over and we are going to list the things you do not like, but we are going to put them down as if they were already corrected. What are the things," I asked him, "that you don't like about your wife?"

Well, this was easy. Right away he could think of quite a few. She was sharp-tongued, impatient, a perfectionist, and on and on and on.

"All right," I said, "let's put down 'I bless you for your patience'."

He looked a little surprised, but he nodded. Then, we put down "I bless you for your tolerance." Third, we put down "I bless you for your easy-going nature." Before we were through he was laughing. "I get the point," he said. "We are going to see her perfect now."

"Right," I said, "and she will feel it if you bless her every day for these points even though they seem hard to realize." This is what I told him to do: Speak her name in your mind each day, morning, noon and night, and then take the first item of the first side of the sheet, "Mary, for your neat and tidy appearance I bless you and bless you and bless you, and praise you and praise you and praise you. Mary, for your good housekeeping I bless you and bless you and bless you, and praise you and praise you and praise you." I told him to try to really feel the blessing as he went along, to really love her for these good points. After he had finished blessing her for the points on the first side of the sheet, he was to turn it over and take the points where he was to see her as already perfect, such as, "Mary, for your loving, patient nature I bless you and bless you and bless you, and praise you and praise you and praise you. For the love that you show to me I bless you and bless you and bless you, and praise you and praise you and praise you."

Well, he agreed that he would try my Blessing Technique

and not tell anyone about it. He would try it for a week and let me know at the end of the week what happened.

Now I thought, this is where the real challenge comes in. If I can just sell Mary on the same idea we'll have something going here. Imagine my surprise when we came out of my office to find that Mary was smiling. In fact, she looked a little like the cat that had swallowed the canary. She and my wife were laughing and talking and I soon sensed that it would not be necessary to talk to Mary at all, for she was smiling at her husband, and they went out happily together.

After they had left my wife said, "What do you know? It just came to me to tell Mary about the Blessing Technique and she agreed to try it for a week and not tell him anything about it."

Then we sat down and had a good laugh together. Unbeknownst to each other, we had both described to this couple the Blessing Technique! This was on a Monday afternoon and we prayed for them during the week and blessed them, too. You can picture our joy, the following Sunday, to see them coming down the street to church hand in hand.

Is there someone in your life who is hard for you to love? Perhaps you think of this person as a difficult person, a problem person. Try the Blessing Technique. You will be amazed at the result. Make yourself a blessing treatment just as we did for the young husband in the story I just told you. Take a clean sheet of paper and write down on one side all of the things you can like and admire about that person. On the other side of the sheet transpose all of the things you find hard to like in the person—that is, if the person seems stingy, write down: "Your generous nature"; if the person seems to have a bad temper, write down: "Your good natured disposition," etc. Then, several times each day speak the person's name in your mind and take the various items on each side of the sheet and bless him or her. Say in your mind: "For the love that you share with others, I bless you and bless you and bless you, I praise you and praise you and praise you." Try to feel the words so that you create an aura of love for this person. I guarantee if you are faithful in using the Blessing Technique that something wonderful will happen.

In the first place you, yourself, will feel better. You will stop struggling in your mind with this "difficult person." You will feel uplifted, happy, free of the problem, and you will really be surprised at the way your feeling is transferred to the one who seemed to you to be hard to love. This is a wonderful treatment to use in connection with our children, our in-laws, and the troublesome people we sometimes find in the office.

Let me tell you another story about someone who used the Blessing Technique. A friend of ours worked in a large office. In this office there was one woman who was so difficult that she was generally disliked by everyone else who worked there, a person who seemed to be so filled with hate that she was venomous. Everyone in the office felt it to the point where they all hated to go to work. We will call this woman Evelyn (this of course was not her real name). She was the bookkeeper in the company and her desk was set aside by a sort of open grill work which gave her the appearance of being in a cage. When you opened the door of the office in the morning you could feel hate vibrations coming out of this cage to meet you. The salesmen used to joke about her and say laughingly to each other, "Throw her a piece of red meat, boys, she's a raging tiger today!" My friend who told me this story, like the others in the office, had built up a strong resistance to Evelyn. But my friend was a truth student, and I prevailed upon her to try using the Blessing Technique.

One morning in her meditation she said she remembered the words of Paul in 1 Cor., *I show you a more excellent way.* "Why that's the Blessing Technique," she thought. "Love is the more excellent way." And so she worked out a blessing treatment such as the one I have just described to you, and promised herself, "I'm going to try loving Evelyn." And she did just that. In order to do this, she really had to discipline her mind. She called it "The Blessing Evelyn Program." Just as the young couple had done, she made a list of all of the things that were most hateful about Evelyn — her antagonistic approach to people; her way of scolding the other employees; her dishonesty; her cheating, etc., etc. Then, she took each one of the items on her list and translated them into positive ideas.

Her blessing program went something like this: every morning when she got out her list to bless Evelyn she would say: "Evelyn, for your wonderful, generous nature, I bless you and bless you and bless you; for the love and understanding that you show all of us, I bless you and praise you and praise you and praise you; for your patience, for your honesty, for the spirit of truth within you, I bless you and bless you, and praise you and praise you and praise you." My friend said this was not easy. It took a lot of doing! But she kept it up for a week. At the end of the week she said she really didn't know whether *she* had changed or *Evelyn* had changed, but she felt much better and she could see that the entire atmosphere in the office had improved. In the first place she discovered that she no longer hated to go to work.

"Well," she thought, "I'll keep it up for another week and just see what happens."

A miracle took place. At the end of the second week my friend went to work on a Monday morning and was greeted by Evelyn with a *warm, loving smile.* You've heard it said "A leopard doesn't change its spots." This one did. Actually this was the first time in months that anyone had seen Evelyn smile, and really the first time she had smiled at my friend. Evelyn beckoned her over to her "cage" and held up a book she was reading. It was a book by Emmet Fox entitled *The Sermon on the Mount.* She said, "I am reading the most wonderful book. I wonder if you can tell me where I can find more like it?" To make a long story short, Evelyn became deeply interested in our philosophy and as she studied this new approach to life she became completely transformed. She began to attend my lectures and was the means of many other people attending my lectures. People who had witnessed this remarkable change in Evelyn wanted to find out what had caused it.

Here's another story that will interest you. The man who told me this story told me to feel free to use it. His name was Dick and he was the manager of the men's department in a large department store. He knew the business from A to Z. However, his department showed very little profit. He and the general manager, it turned out, had a deep-seated resentment for each other. Periodically, Dick would make a list of the merchandise he wanted to buy for his department. He then would take it to the general manager for his O.K. The general manager would glare at the list and then start to pare it down, so that even if everything on the list were to be sold out there would still be a bare profit.

Dick was frustrated. In fact, he was desperate when he told me his story. I heard him out, and then, remembering how well the Blessing Technique had worked for others, I told him about it. He agreed that someone would have to break the chain of hate and that he would have to be that someone. So together we set up a blessing treatment for the general manager, whom we will call Bill. Soon Dick said he began to realize that when he passed Bill in the office he no longer tried to avoid him; in fact, he felt different about Bill. He began to see that Bill, too, had a lot of problems, and that no doubt he (Dick) was one of them. As his attitude gradually changed, Dick noticed that at staff meetings Bill would sometimes smile his way. This, formerly, had never been the case.

The next time he took his list of merchandise to be O.K.'d by Bill, Bill signed it with hardly a glance at it. And then he looked up at Dick and said: "Dick, I do not understand it. I used to hate you with a passion. I just don't know. Either I have changed or you've changed."

Shortly after this episode the firm opened a new branch store and at the suggestion of Bill they made Dick the general manager, a real promotion. As a sidelight to this story I would like to add that when Dick first came to my lectures he told me that he came because he wanted to earn $25,000 a year. Somebody told him that if he studied my teaching he would be able to earn $25,000 a year. I told him he had come to the wrong place, that our philosophy was not a get-rich-quick-scheme. Later he told me he had come to the right place. In his new position he was paid $25,000 a year, which was a very handsome salary at that time.

The seventh technique on our Love Technique list is similar to the sixth. Here is number seven:

VII. Use the "I Love You—I Understand You"
Technique Whenever There Is a Misunderstanding
Between You and Another.

As you can see, this is really a continuation of number six,
but it is more of a "quickie" treatment. Never let a
misunderstanding grow. When there is a misunderstanding
between you or another, when you are tempted to be ir-
ritated or resentful toward another, think in your mind "I
love you. (And speak the person's name.) I understand you."
And then reverse it. "Mary loves me, Mary understands
me."

We live in a mental world, as Emmet Fox said many times,
and our feelings are known to the other person in the one
mind. You have the choice. You can build up a feeling of
resentment and irritation that will be felt by the other, or
you can build up a circle of love that will bring peace and
harmony into the situation. Try these two techniques. Practice on the people in your life who seem hardest to love. You
will be amazed at the great return that will be yours. You
will receive back so much more than you gave that it will
be well worth the trouble and the discipline.

It is like the story of St. Francis and the leper. St. Francis
loathed the leper. He could not bear to see him, and then
one day love caused him to put his arms around the leper.
He kissed the leper right on his sores, and when he did so
the leper was healed. Sometimes the blessing, forgiving
technique seems as hard to us as it was for St. Francis to kiss
the leper, but as we mentally "kiss the leper" he is healed and
we are healed in the process.

In our next chapter we will continue with more love
techniques.

Your Statement of Love

The Kingdom of Heaven is at hand. I am free to experience it the moment I free others. I serve my fellow man by releasing him to his own highest good. I release the past, knowing that Principle is not bound by precedent. No condition of the past has power over me. I release my children, freeing them to grow and express in their own individual ways. I release my friends from any confining thoughts I may have had about them.

Since the creative word of life is constantly recreating the world, I know that yesterday's failure is today's success. Everywhere I look I see the life of God made manifest. I see the wholeness of God in every physical body and this wholeness is reflected in me. I feel the love of God in every human heart and according to the Law of Life, this is the love I am able to receive in my life. I become free by freeing others, and for this I am most grateful. And so it is.

—*Your Needs Met*, p. 127.

12

LOVE—THE ANSWER TO EVERY NEED

(More Love Techniques)

*First keep the peace within yourself, then you can also
bring peace to others.*

—Thomas à Kempis
The Imitation of Christ

Much is said about the importance of love, but the big
question is how can we learn to love? We learn how to love
by using Love Techniques.

VIII. Forgiveness Technique: Forgive Yourself;
Forgive Others and Forgive God.

Right away several questions come to mind. Why should
we forgive when it's so much fun to have a grudge? Why
forgive when it is inwardly satisfying to hate? Why forgive

when someone has done to you what seems to be an irreparable wrong? We must forgive because without forgiveness there can be no love.

Forgiveness must precede love. Forgiveness is giving up resentment, hate or any such feelings that are contrary to the feeling of love. Forgiveness opens the way for clarity of thinking, for sensible thinking. Now love can come into the picture.

When two people get together to "run down" another, there is low-grade hate at work. People think that it is natural to gossip about others, but gossip is resentment in which two people are in common agreement. It seems to be a natural thing but really love is the natural thing.

Sometimes it builds the ego to find someone we think is worse than we are. In reading the newspaper we are continually setting ourselves up as being "good" in comparison to others who are doing "foul deeds." Again hate is running rampant.

We love only when we are able to recognize the good in others, to affirm the good, and to love the good. When we do this, we are able to overlook the bad and not give power to that which seems to be evil. In his letter to the Philippians Paul gave us our technique. He said, *Whatsoever things are true, whatsoever things are honest, whatsoever things are just, whatsoever things are pure, whatsoever things are lovely, whatsoever things are of good report; if there be any virtue, and if there be any praise, think on these things.*[1] It is interesting that the foregoing is followed by this statement: *And the God of peace shall be with you.*[2] Let your conversation be in "heaven." Whenever we have something to say about another, if it isn't

[1]Phil. 4:8.
[2]Phil. 4:9.

in accord with Paul's admonition, then it is better unsaid. Then we will have less to forgive ourselves for.

Guilt is dependent upon condemnation of the self. When we feel guilty we are condemning the self. When we condemn others, we also condemn ourselves. This is the reason we feel out of harmony with life after we have indulged in a "gossip" session, or when we have spent time maligning another, accusing him or her in our hearts of evil things. Nothing is going to be gained by condemning others; the only one who is hurt is the one who does the condemning.

Why forgive? It is imperative that we forgive if we want to have peace of mind. Condemnation only hurts the one condemning and not the one condemned. Hate is like a bonfire; it scorches the ground upon which it burns. Hate hardens the heart in which it is allowed to rest. Hate interferes with creativity. It blocks the ability to think clearly and causes good thoughts to go out the window.

The reason that Jesus was so effective as a teacher and healer was because he based everything that he did on love. He said, *Judge not that ye be not judged, for with what judgment ye judge, ye shall be judged; and with what measure ye mete, it shall be measured to you again.*[3] We judge others and then have to forgive our own judgments. Righteous judgment means to look through the appearances, to look through the apparent evil, to look through the hate, and to recognize that each and every person is centered in love. Just as water poured into a pump will act as a primer to cause water to flow, love poured into a situation will act as a primer. Look at the person who seems hard to love and silently affirm: "The Christ in me salutes the Christ in you."

It is fruitless to think that we can overcome hate with hate.

[3]Mt. 7:1,2.

Hate will beget hate unless the chain of hate is broken by love. If we persist with love, it will eventually overcome hate.

Jesus said, *Ye have heard that it hath been said, Thou shalt love thy neighbor, and hate thine enemy. But I say unto you, Love your enemies, bless them that curse you, do good to them that hate you, and pray for them which despitefully use you.*[4] This is the key to the way it works. Always feel that you can forgive irrespective of what may have been the provocation for hate. Forgive and release, and you will find that love will prevail.

Peter approached Jesus and asked how many times should one forgive, seven times? Jesus replied, *Seventy times seven.*[5] Mathematically you would say this meant four hundred and ninety, but the term *seven* means infinite perfection. Seventy times seven is a scriptural device for emphasis. It means to forgive and forgive and forgive on into infinity until the spiritual perfection is realized.

One time a man came to see me who was having difficulty with certain people in his office. He was tempted to fire them all, but he wanted to try something different. So he forgave them over and over, each time substituting love for the resentment and appearances of hate. Eventually, when he was able to prove love to them through his actions the whole situation clarified. These people became trusted, loyal and loving employees who appreciated him.

When we first started our prison work at Folsom Prison in California we received a letter from one of the prisoners in which he said that the book of ours which helped him the most was *The Truth About Emotional Maturity*. He wrote

[4]Mt. 5:43,44.
[5]Mt. 18:22.

that the biggest problem among prisoners was self-forgiveness: "They all hate themselves." He said that once he had learned to forgive himself he found it became easy to forgive others and to forgive life. I continually emphasize the need among prisoners to forgive themselves first, recognizing the truth of their own being, and being aware of the Spirit of God indwelling them. I try to show them what this can mean, the immensity of such a realization, how it will open up a whole new vista of understanding and an entirely new way of life. This, I am happy to say, has been proven in our work with the various prisons.

Just recently I received a letter from a prisoner in the Atlanta federal penitentiary. He writes: "I notice that the Folsom program already bears good fruit. It is the very best type of program for prisoners. More than most, they suffer from a screaming case of low self-worth and have made any number of incorrect identifications of self."

Forgiveness is not a sign of weakness, but of strength. It takes a strong person to be willing to say, "Irrespective of what you have done to me or to someone I love, I forgive you."

There have been many instances where teenagers have gotten a great satisfaction out of being hostile. Yet, when they were faced with love there was something within them that responded, causing the hate and the hostility to be stilled.

The key is "It doesn't matter what's done to me, it's how I take it." How do we react? Do we retain our own individuality, our own thoughts, our own strength, or do we react by entering into the hate program? Having compassion means to understand that the other person is doing what he is doing because he thinks it is best under the circumstances. Love is contagious, and love is able to overcome any obstacle.

IX. Look for Things to Praise and Give Recognition of the Good in Others.

Praising and raising go hand in hand. When you praise someone, your affirmation of them raises them up in their own esteem and a bond is formed. It is easy to love through praise because one is then finding good in the person, and this good becomes more pronounced and accessible through praise. Conversely, condemnation tears down and eventually destroys.

Praise builds up. Praise your wife for the way she keeps house, or for the way she dresses, or for the many good things that she does. Make it a point to eliminate condemnation. The area of good that is being praised will spread, and there will be less to condemn until eventually all sense of condemnation will be eradicated through the constructive, dynamic and loving use of praise.

Praise your husband. Recognize the good in him and praise it. Praise him for working hard, trying to make more than just a living for the family. Praise him for his kindness to you and to others. Praise him for the way he combs his hair, or for the way he dresses. Praise him for his interest in golf. Instead of condemnation, substitute praise, and you will find that his attitude toward you and the family will change. Praise is founded upon love. Through love we see only the good, and this good becomes magnified and grows through praise.

Praise your employees for the work they are doing. Praise

them for the little things that they do beyond the scope of their employment. Praise them for their good attitudes, and for the good feeling that they engender with clients and customers. In turn, if you are an employee, praise your employer for his generosity, and for his fairness. Find various things for which you can praise him to other people. Create an atmosphere in your own mind of praise for your employer and your daily work will become a joy rather than a drudgery. There is a raising up through praising, and you will raise your own consciousness, and your own feeling of well-being through praising those with whom you daily come in contact.

Praise your country. This is a wonderful country. This country has the biggest heart of any country in the world. More people help other people in this country than anywhere else. This country needs to be built up rather than torn down. It can be built up through praise. Praise the officials, and the police, and the various people who are endeavoring to make this society work. Praise them, and you will find that the attitude of these people toward others will change. Praise raises consciousness.

The book of Psalms is a book of praise. *Praise ye the Lord* is said over and over. All right! *Praise ye the Lord.* Praise the Power of God right within you. Praise the love of God living through you. Praise the goodness of God which surrounds you. Praise the peace of God which fills you. Praise God over and over, every day. This is an easy way to build a consciousness of the awareness of the presence of God.

Take a walk and sing these words to the cadence of your steps: *I AM FILLED WITH THE LIFE OF GOD, AND UPHELD BY HIS YOUNG, JOYFUL SPIRIT FOREVER.* As you step along with these words singing in your mind you will feel your whole being lifted up and you will become closer to the Spirit of God within you.

X. Learn to Have Compassion for the Faults in Others.

We all have faults. We all have shortcomings. No one lives up to his full potential. What may be a fault to one person may be an asset to another. No one has the same feelings, and no one recognizes the same needs. Each one is a unique individual. Therefore, when we find a fault in someone else we are reacting to our own faults. If I were to point my finger at you, bear in mind that in doing so I am pointing three fingers at myself. You try it. It makes no difference what another person may be thinking or doing, you will never gain stature by condemning him.

The greatest example of one who insisted on forgiveness without any thought of quibbling was Jesus, who had compassion on those who were crucifying him. He said, *Father forgive them; for they know not what they do.*[6] Can we do less? Have compassion. Love others, and forgive them their faults, because they are doing these things without thinking. Usually, they are doing the best that they can at their point of awareness.

Have compassion for others who think differently than you do. They are not thinking that way just to annoy you. When someone gossips about you, or says malicious things about you, do not become embroiled in controversy. Let them go. If you become emotionally embroiled, you then accept the very faults that you are condemning in them.

Jesus put it another way when Peter complained about

[6]Lk. 23:34.

others. His response was, *What is that to thee? Follow thou me.*[7] The things on the material level which impede our spiritual growth are not for us. We have to turn away from them and know that there is only one power, and that power is God, infinite good, right where we are. We are following the Christ within.

XI. At Every Opportunity Be a Peacemaker.

Do you remember the little statue of the three monkeys— *Hear No Evil, See No Evil, Speak No Evil?* Sometimes we think that following this admonition would cause us to lose the zest in life, but what is the virtue in being involved with evil? Some people think that it is exciting, that it is fun, but we find that it is always heartbreaking, and that the results are something that we would rather have avoided. By seeing evil, we accept evil into our own consciousness. When we see what seems to be, or appears to be evil, recognize it for what it is—that it is not the truth, and then mentally reverse it.

You see a person who is letting himself be destroyed by drugs. Look at him, have compassion on him, and realize that he has lost sight of the true self. He is more to be pitied than condemned. Then look beyond this habit and see the spirit of truth within this person. Praise the spirit of truth, and love the God within. Do not accept the habit as being a reality, but accept only the reality of God within him. Know that anything can be overcome through the spirit of truth. As you know the truth about this person, the truth will prevail.

Always seek peace instead of conflict. Always seek har-

[7]Jn. 21:22.

123

mony instead of discord. Peace is within the mind of each person, and the desire for peace is as universal as the desire to breathe. So find the point of harmony and peace within each situation, and let it quell the storm. Speak your word for peace. *My peace I give unto you: not as the world giveth*[8] [for my peace is beyond human understanding.] Think peace, and peace will be your experience. Think love, and love will be your experience.

XII. Living by Grace.

All things work together for good to them that love God.[9] Loving God means to trust God. *Trust in the Lord with all thine heart, and lean not unto thine own understanding. In all thy ways acknowledge him, and he shall direct thy paths.*[10] Once we understand that the power of love, working in and through us, is able to do everything, we see that all things do work together for good when we love God (Love). When our hearts are filled with joy through knowing that right where we are is all of the wonder and glory of life, then our hearts are filled with love. Love is respect for the presence within, the power within, and it is reliance upon the power. Jesus taught how to think right, and this is very essential, but he also taught us to love. He found that through love he was able to accomplish great things that could not be accomplished otherwise. Love is the highest good—the summum bonum.

Living by Grace means living by resting in the wisdom and

[8]Jn. 14:27.
[9]Rom. 8:28.
[10]Prv. 3:6.

power of God, spontaneously expressed right where we are. Grace is the illimitable love of God, living through us. When we live by Grace we are truly living in love.

Your Statement of Love

And when ye stand praying, forgive, if ye have aught against any: that your Father also which is in heaven may forgive you.[11]

Turning from the problems and cares of the day, I now consciously accept the truth about God and myself. I know that God is the only power and the only presence. I know that I am the expression of God and that all the Father hath is mine. I am a divine, perfect, spiritual being, forever one with my source. Turning from problems, I listen in the silence for God's perfect answers. Turning from confusion, I accept the peace that passes all understanding. I let the perfect life of God live through me.

I now release all those who have ever hurt or offended me. I forgive them completely. I forgive myself for the mistakes of the past. Releasing others, I am released. Love is the answer to my every need.

All that I need or desire is right within me. In this moment of silence the work is done. The spirit within me is the substance of all my desires, I joyously and thankfully accept the good I desire for myself and the good I desire for others. That which I realize in the invisible becomes manifest in my world. Forgiveness has opened the door to divine right action in my world. And so it is.

—*Your Needs Met*, p. 65.

[11]Mk. 11:25.

13

LOVE TRANSCENDS GUILTS

---

*Finish every day and be done with it. You have done
what you could. Some blunders and absurdities no doubt
crept in; forget them as soon as you can. Tomorrow is a
new day; begin it well and serenely and with too high a
spirit to be cumbered with your old nonsense. This day is
all that is good and fair. It is too dear, with its hopes and
invitations, to waste a moment on the yesterdays.*
—Ralph Waldo Emerson

During the many years that we have been in this work,
we have talked to many people. Probably hundreds of them
have told us that they were suffering from guilt feelings that
should have been released and forgotten years ago. Guilt is
a remorseful awareness of having done something wrong. It
is a feeling of shame or fault over some past event or thought
or feeling about life. Guilt is pure self-condemnation which
harms the person who harbors it. It should be dispelled, the
originating mistake forgiven and the whole matter released
as soon as possible.

WHERE INNOCENCE WAS BLISS

The opposite of guilt is to be guiltless which is to be free from guilt, innocent. The Garden of Eden story in Genesis brings this out so cleverly. Adam and Eve were completely innocent until they ate (accepted for themselves) the fruit of the tree of the knowledge of good and evil. Which is to say they partook of human judgment. The allegory tells us that they immediately realized that they were naked and were so ashamed that they tried to cover their nakedness. It was the guilt of judgment that took them sorrowfully out of Paradise and caused them to be guilt ridden forevermore along with all their descendants.

Guilt will do it every time. Guilt denies the perfect life of God within us. Guilt causes us to feel separated from the love of God. And when you look at it this way, it becomes the "original sin" for every sin (mistake) stems from a sense of separation from God, our very life.

HOW GUILT BEGINS

Each person has a built-in conscience which acts as a teacher, teaching him right from wrong. When that teacher is disregarded or suppressed through rationalization, there arises a sense of guilt. For instance, it is not natural to tell a lie. The first time it is done the conscience will come into play. At that time it has to be brushed off, disregarded, in order for the person to be able to go ahead with the lie. This provokes a feeling of guilt and uneasiness that must then be suppressed. If the person continues to tell lies, the conscience will continually be suppressed until the person will not know the difference between a lie and a true statement. Even so, subjectively the guilt feeling is there.

Sometimes guilt arises through conduct that causes shame. Many people have been taught that sex is dirty and shameful. Parents sometimes teach this to their children in order to keep them from having sex experience before they are married. This deep sense of shame continues ever after with every sex experience and, even after marriage, can cause frigidity and impotence in a subconscious effort to refrain from the shameful act. This has caused many marriages to fail that would have been perfect otherwise.

Sex is by no means the only ground for producing guilt feelings. There are so many areas we could not possibly list them all. However, here are a few of the most common guilt producers.

A surprising number of people have a guilt about receiving money. Somewhere along the line they have accepted the idea that it is virtuous to be poor. Because of this deep-seated guilt about money they tend to push it away. Therefore, they are reduced to poverty and continue in that state throughout their lives.

Many hang onto a sense of guilt about some unkindness, some oversight where a friend or relative was neglected or hurt by a thoughtless act on their part years before. Perhaps through some unintentional misdeed another was harmed, or some act of negligence caused an injury to another. This causes the "guilty" person to lie awake nights regretting the unfortunate incident.

A common cause of guilt stems out of the desire on the part of a child to please the parent. Some children never succeed in pleasing their parents. Thus many guilts arise from the parent-child relationship.

A TRUE STORY ABOUT HOW
ONE WOMAN PUNISHED HERSELF

One time a woman came to us who was suffering from chronic insomnia. For thirty years, she had had trouble sleeping. When she went to bed at night, just as she would start to drift off into sleep, she would immediately awaken with a start and begin thinking uneasily and guiltily about a past event. This would go on through the night. Eventually she would get up and walk around the house in an endeavor to stay awake the rest of the night. She had tried sleeping pills, relaxing exercises and meditation but nothing seemed to help. As we talked, she went back into her life and told us of an incident that had occurred the night that her mother died.

She was a young lady at the time, the sole support of her mother and herself when her mother became seriously ill with a lingering illness. Friends and relatives living nearby came in during the day to look after mother but when the daughter came home in the evening it was up to her to nurse her mother from then on. She would feed her and prepare her for the night and then try to get a little sleep herself. But, over and over during the night her mother would call her and she would have to wake up and do some little chore for her like getting her a glass of water, closing the window, etc. This went on for months until eventually the daughter was completely worn out. The mother got worse as time went on and it became apparent that this was going to be her last illness.

One night the daughter was awakened from a deep sleep. Half awake, she faintly heard her mother calling. She was so weary from lack of sleep night after night that she just couldn't rouse herself. She drifted back into sleep. The next thing she knew it was morning. It was nearly noon and there was an unnatural stillness in the house. She felt refreshed. It was the first night's sleep she'd had in months. And then she remembered her mother. She ran to her mother's room and found that mother had passed away during the night.

From that moment on she believed that her sleepiness had caused her mother to die. It must have been her fault. If only she hadn't gone back to sleep! If only she had gone and helped her mother, maybe her mother wouldn't have died. People tried to talk to her telling her that mother was going to die anyway. What difference did it make whether she died that night or the next night. This was cold comfort to our friend. She continued to feel that it was her fault that her mother had passed on and had difficulty sleeping from then on. The feeling of guilt diminished somewhat over the years, and yet she had never been able to get rid of insomnia. Mother had now been gone for over thirty years and still she walked the floor or read detective stories through the night. When daylight came she would fall into a fitful sleep.

Finally one day she asked, "How can I get rid of the deep-seated feeling of guilt I have about mother? I can talk myself out of it during the daylight hours but at night it is always there with the darkness. How can I develop a new attitude?"

As we talked together about this uneasy feeling that haunted her every night, she began to see that she was punishing herself by not letting herself fall asleep. Subconsciously, she was trying to make it up to mother. She was mentally beating herself with her self-imposed guilt. She didn't have to keep it. Mother had long since forgiven her and God had never condemned her. We talked about eternal life and pictured mother happy in her new experience. We told her that we forgave her and we had a prayer together asking God to forgive her.

As she left, she told us that she felt as if a huge burden had slipped from her shoulders. The next morning she called to tell us that she had slept the night through for the first time in thirty years.

THE WORLD ACCEPTS US AT OUR OWN EVALUATION

This story may sound extreme, but you'd be surprised how many people are lying awake nights because they haven't been able to forgive themselves for some past mistake, some oversight, some failure to live up to the high standards they had set up for themselves. Long after we have been able to forgive everyone else in our experience we find that we are still holding out on ourselves. Having learned to be tolerant of everyone else, we still set up for ourselves impossible goals of perfection, mentally lashing ourselves over and over again for what we, ourselves, judge to be failures.

The world will take you at your own evaluation still holds true. When we cannot forgive ourselves, the world accepts us as falling short. No one attains emotional maturity without self-acceptance. It is the most important step of all, achieved only after we are able to forgive ourselves for past mistakes or failures.

GETTING RID OF GUILTS

Do you have trouble forgiving yourself? Do you ever wake up in the night feeling guilty about some past mistake? Do you long to do it all over again in order to correct the unhappy past? Well, you can. You can reconstruct the past and mentally erase the dark places. Remember what Jesus said to the woman taken in adultery? He said, *Neither do I condemn thee: go, and sin no more.* We have all made mistakes, but it is not required of us that we pay over and over throughout the years for some mistake in the past. It only serves to make us ill and keeps our present good from coming to us. Many a person has found that he or she recovers from some persistent illness after being able to forgive the self or another. Much of our illness is a form of self-punishment. Let us resolve right now to be through with this kind of destructive thinking. The answer is: *Forgive the self for every destructive thought or act and forgive others for every hurt or wrong that has been done you.* It is just not worth it to carry this debris around. We must wipe the slate clean and start over.

LOVE IS THE ANSWER

Love erases the hurts of the past. Just as love overcomes fear, so does love overcome misery and despair. Mentally say to the person who has hurt you, "Mary, I love you and understand you. I forgive you freely." Now, don't you feel better? In the same way forgive yourself. Know that you did the best you could at the time. Even though the person

132

whom you unwittingly hurt may have gone on, silently address that person. "I love you, Mary (John or whoever), I did not mean to hurt you. I now make amends by giving you an extra measure of love." Now forgive yourself completely and vow never to dig up the old guilt again.

We were talking about self-punishment. You'd be surprised how common this is. Many times we actually draw some misery to ourselves because subconsciously we want to punish ourselves for something we think we should not have done. Long after we have forgotten the cause we continue to produce in our bodies the effects we have subconsciously drawn to ourselves. Ask yourself, "Am I suffering from some ailment that has been brought about in this manner?" Perhaps you have been holding a grudge that you would be happier and healthier without, perhaps you have been holding a grudge against yourself. Ask God to reveal to you any hidden guilts or grudges and then make a point of erasing them. If necessary write them down and burn the paper afterward. Do whatever will make you feel that these old dark spots have been completely wiped out. The past must be forgiven before a person can accept a healing.

FORGIVING THE SELF

We knew a man who went through all sorts of tortures year after year after year. Why? Because, once when he was playing trumpet in an orchestra, he sounded off on some sour notes. He never wanted to play the trumpet again. He couldn't face the other members of the orchestra, let alone the conductor. He put aside his trumpet. He never touched it again. In order to escape from his thoughts about himself he started drinking. He drank for years. Well on the way to wasting his entire life, he finally had it pointed out to him that he just had to release that old mistake, that it really wasn't anything, certainly not important enough to punish himself for an entire lifetime. Finally, he was able to forgive himself and start a new life.

There are many degrees of self-condemnation. Not every guilt takes such a toll, but every guilt is self-destructive. Many a person destroys himself because subconsciously he is punishing himself for something he felt he did wrong years ago. Let us be done with this destructive thinking.

Forgive yourself. Right this moment is the cut-off time. Forgive yourself for past mistakes. Give up the grudge you carry against yourself. God has forgiven you long ago, even before you made the mistake. Forgive yourself and start a fresh new experience. Here is a treatment for you to use. This may be the clue you seek as to why your prayers have not been answered. Many have opened the door to a whole series of healings by forgiving themselves.

Your Statement of Love

Neither do I condemn thee: go, and sin no more.[1]

Any sense of separation from God is a sin. I have made many mistakes in the past. I have "sinned" against myself and others. To continue to have remorse and guilt over these mistakes is to continue to separate myself from God. This is the greatest mistake of all.

[1]Jn. 8:11.

I now forgive myself for every past mistake. All condemnation is released. I give up every destructive feeling about the past, every feeling of separateness. I let go of all resentment, every hate and fear. God knows nothing about sin for He did not create it. The Christ within me has never been contaminated. In Truth, I have never been separated from God for a single instant.

Divine Love at the center of my being frees me from any sense of condemnation of myself and others. As I forgive, I am freely forgiven. I am made free through the Christ. *In Christ I am a new creation.* I let go of the past. I have no guilt regarding the past and no apprehension for the future. I am free. And so it is.

—*Your Needs Met*, p. 66.

CHAPTER
14

THE OVERVIEW

1. God and love are synonymous.

2. Love is the greatest power there is, a power to which nothing is impossible.

3. Love is omnipresent (everywhere present), omnipotent (all powerful) and omniscient (all knowing).

4. Love is the energy within all of life.

5. Each person is a center of infinite love.

6. Through recognition, the use of infinite love within a person can grow.

7. Love is expressed in feeling, thought and action.

8. The easiest way to love is to recognize love at the center of one's being; become immersed in that love; then in

your imagination draw a circle around that love. Next think of someone you would like to love, maybe someone you have hated in the past; draw a larger circle in your mind and take that person in. Keep drawing larger and larger circles taking in others.

9. As you use love it grows until eventually you have established a love consciousness. This is the commandment of Jesus, to *love one another* without judgment.

10. There is no power in hate; there is no power in fear; there is no power in anxiety; there is only power in love.

11. When you cannot find the solution to a problem, usually the missing ingredient is love.

12. None of us will ever achieve emotional maturity until we have learned to love not only our neighbor but ourselves.

13. When Gautama the Buddha sat under the Bo tree he made the great discovery, *Only love goes from me and only love comes to me.*

14. The love we realize within ourselves and pass on to others will bring sanity to a disturbed world.

15. Love, being omnipresent, is the common denominator of all life. As we express love we immediately find that we have something very definite in common with every part of life.

16. There are no barriers where love is the bridge.

17. A lack of love in the heart is a sense of separation from God.

18. *Beloved, let us love one another, for love is of God; and everyone who loves is born of God and knows God. He who does not love does not know God, for God is love.* (1 John 4:7,8 New KJV)

19. It is as impossible to define love as it is to define the infinite—for love is infinite.

20. Love can heal a sick body; love can make friends out of enemies; love can cause a failing business to prosper.

21. Love could erase all crime, conflict and war from the world.

22. There is no condition—no matter how fixed and intolerable—which cannot be overcome by love.

23. People since time began have been looking for a panacea, a universal remedy or a cure-all, for their bodily ills and for world problems. There is such a panacea. It is love.

24. Love is the highest emotion or feeling that can be experienced.

25. Love is the energy which created the universe.

26. Love is God affirming His creation and calling it good; never condemning; never denying the existence of good.

27. Love continually forgives because love never has judged nor condemned in the first place.

28. To understand love is to understand life.

29. *We love because he first loved us.* (1 John 4:19 RSV)

30. Where there is a lack of love, life becomes diminished. We live in proportion to our love.

31. We hate only that which we fear. Perfect love casts out fear and neutralizes hate.

32. *The fruit of the spirit is love.* (Gal. 5:22 RSV)

33. *Love is the fulfilling of the law.* (Rom. 13:10 RSV)

34. The brotherhood of man is bound together by love.

35. Through love the paradox occurs that two beings become one and yet remain two.

36. We do not have to generate love or make love happen; it is the gift of God.

37. If you are searching for the right job, for the right house, for the right companion, stop. Let love go before you to prepare the way, to bring light on the pathway; love can do it when nothing else can.

38. The late Emmet Fox gave us this powerful statement:

There is no difficulty that enough love will not conquer; no disease that enough love will not heal; no door
that enough love will not open; no gulf that enough
love will not bridge; no wall that enough love will not
throw down; no sin that enough love will not redeem.
It makes no difference how deeply seated may be the
trouble, how hopeless the outlook, how muddled the
tangle, how great the mistake: a sufficient realization of
love will dissolve it all. If only you could love enough
you would be the happiest and most powerful being in
the world.

39. *And above all these put on love, which binds everything
    together in perfect harmony.* (Col. 3:14 RSV)

40. Pitirim A. Sorokin said:
    Now more than ever before I believe the following
    truths, which are fully confirmed by our experimental
    studies: hate begets hate, violence engenders violence,
    hypocrisy is answered by hypocrisy, war generates war
    and love creates love.

41. Indifference is hate and love caught at a crossroads.
    Never let it rest there. Break the impasse with love.

42. Pseudo-love is not real love. On the human level we are
    inclined to confuse our terms. The way we often use the
    word *love* shows how little many of us know about it.
    We say: "I love oranges; I love my sports car; I love
    baseball and I love my wife." We use the same word. Do
    we mean the same thing? How often we use the word
    love when we mean "I desire; I want to possess; I get
    gratification from; I exploit; or, I feel guilty about"!

140

43. Other forms of pseudo-love:

    (a) Overindulgence of children stemming from selfish pride.

    (b) Overprotection of one's wife, or others, out of fear.

    (c) Possessive feelings and actions akin to jealousy.

    (d) Self-sacrificing to get attention as a martyr.

    (e) Sentimental love to gain recognition and acclaim.

    (f) Idolatrous love marked by excessive adoration and deification of another human being.

    (g) Love of power; love of possessions; love of money; are all forms of self-aggrandizement.

44. When we measure love we are almost sure to be disappointed.

45. It is not what is done to us that matters, but how do we react? Do we react in love?

46. One cannot control the words or thoughts of another; but, one can control one's own thoughts and responses.

47. People spend their lives trying to get love when the only love they can ever know is the love they experience within, the love they give to others.

48. It is easy to love those who love you. The challenge is to love your enemies.

49. To love is not to count the cost but to give freely with no strings attached. Impersonal love does not say, "I will love you if you will love me in return," but loves freely and asks no reward or recognition.

50. TLC has healed more people than all of our sophisticated medications put together. TLC means *tender, loving care.*

51. Today doctors agree that love can cure the sick. They actually prescribe TLC.

52. A famous doctor wrote, *As I look back over the long, full years, one truth emerges clearly in my mind—the universal need for love. Whether they think they do or not, all people want love.*

53. People cannot survive without love; they must have it or they will perish.

54. Perfect love is so impelling no one can resist it.

55. It is not the object of hate that is causing the hate or a resentful person causing the resentment. It is the absence of love.

56. *For God has not given us a spirit of fear, but of power and of love and a sound mind.* (2 Tim. 1:7, New KJV)

57. Love has to begin right within us. Each one has to make a move, be it ever so slight, in the direction of love.

58. The word *compassion* is derived from the root meaning, *with love.*

59. To love is to partake of the very nature of God, to be one with God.

60. Love is the greatest word in any language. Love is universal.

61. Valuable Love Techniques you can use:

(a) Practice receiving love from the infinite source.

(b) Speak love in your mind until you feel it for yourself and for others.

(c) Bless your mind and body daily.

(d) Love the power of love within you—this is loving God within.

(e) Recognizing God in His creation about us is a wonderful way to develop a consciousness of love

(f) Use the "Blessing Technique" for those who seem hard to love.

(g) Use the "I love you—I understand you" technique whenever there is a misunderstanding between you and others.

(h) Use the "Forgiveness Technique"; Forgive yourself; forgive others and forgive God.

(i) Look for things to bless and give recognition of the good in others.

(j) Learn to have compassion for the faults of others.

(k) At every opportunity be a peacemaker.

(l) Living by Grace means resting in the wisdom and power of God, the illimitable love of God, living through us.

62. Perfect love transcends guilts.

63. Love erases the hurts of the past.

ABOUT THE AUTHORS

For more than thirty years the Addingtons have worked closely together in the fields of writing and lecturing. Through its monthly publication, the Abundant Living magazine, Abundant Living Foundation brings its teaching to thousands of people throughout the world.

Jack Addington attended the University of Florida at Gainesville, and has had three successful careers, first in business where he was a practicing attorney, then twenty years in the ministry, founding two large churches. In 1969 he retired from the church to begin his worldwide ministry. He now devotes his time to writing, lecturing, a large radio and prayer ministry, and his work in the prisons.

Cornelia Addington attended the University of Washington in Seattle where she majored in painting and design. She was successful as a designer for a large manufacturing firm, later going into interior design. During the past thirty years she has edited Dr. Addington's manuscripts and co-authored six of his books. She is the editor of the Abundant Living magazine and has had numerous articles published in national magazines.